EXIT
STAGE RIGHT

EXIT
STAGE RIGHT

Conversations
about the Drama of
Finishing Strong & Dying Well

Darrel Gilbertson & Lynn Anderson

LEAFWOOD
PUBLISHERS
Abilene, TX

EXIT STAGE RIGHT

Conversations about the Drama of Finishing Strong & Dying Well

LEAFWOOD
PUBLISHERS

ISBN 978-0-89112-573-0

Printed in the United States of America

Cover design by
Interior text design by Sandy Armstrong

For information contact:
Leafwood Publishers, Abilene, Texas
1-877-816-4455 toll free
www.leafwoodpublishers.com

08 09 10 11 12 13 14 / 7 6 5 4 3 2 1

To loving parents now in glory, and to a family—especially my wife Barbara—so rich in merit and vibrant in their pursuit of life and its joys, I dedicate my efforts in this book.

—Darrel Gilbertson

To "Miss T" (Lillian M. Torkelson) teacher and mentor in my pivotal high school years. You finished strong—spreading hope and encouragement to the end. And you died well—last year at 94.

—Lynn Anderson

Foreword

I.

The United States is a youth-oriented society that is hesitant to talk about death. We admire the characteristics of youth and go to great lengths to deny that we are getting older. Eventually, though, we are confronted with our own mortality. For some, it comes on the heels of a medical diagnosis while others are reminded by the number of candles on their birthday cake. Either way, we are all terminal. Thus, the question is not "will you die" but "what are you supposed to do while you are dying"?

Philosophers, theologians, behavioral scientists, and others have wrestled with this question for centuries and have left an abundance of stage theories and philosophies in their wake. While each is valuable in its own right, the dying experience is a truly unique one that often defies the most well developed theory. It is a time of emotion, reflection, and evaluation as the dying individual assesses his or her past and contemplates the future. "Exit Stage Right" is designed to assist in this process. While theoretically sound, the brilliance of the book is that it is not written exclusively for an academic audience, though both authors have advanced degrees in their fields. Instead, it skillfully balances theory with the human experience by inviting the reader to share in the conversation between two veteran pastors. One (Lynn Anderson) contributes a pragmatic perspective rich with an emphasis on personal experience, while the other (Darrel Gilbertson) brings a more existential slant informed by the major thinkers to the dialogue.

As if moving through the acts of a drama, Lynn and Darrel explore questions that are vital to the human experience such as suffering, relationships, and dying. They discuss the journey of life and the quest for S-aging that requires one to confront the issues of mortality, identity, and legacy. And, most importantly, they consider these matters within the context of Darrel's terminal illness.

As the curtain falls on each act, the authors invite you to join them in the performance by considering your role in the drama of life and evaluating your performance thus far. In addition, they encourage you to write the script for the acts that are yet to come by pondering the deeper issues of life that go beyond promotion, consumption, and accumulation.

"Exit Stage Right" will change the way you view the dying process and, in so doing, will change the way you view life. I am confident that you will find this book to be unique in its approach, engaging in its style, and transforming in its content.

James L. Knapp, Professor of Sociology
Southeastern Oklahoma State University, Durant
Author of *The Graying of the Flock* (2003)

II.

The distilled essence of this marvelous book is this: *Silence is our enemy. Transparency our gift.*

Darrel and Lynn ask us to pull up a chair to their years of deep conversations about topics most of us avoid: dying and death. And those conversations are peppered with thought-provoking quotes, a sprinkle of humor, and intense transparency from these two very different—and very similar—ministers.

Read this book, and you'll be caught up in the script of a play being staged. More importantly, you'll also be gently but firmly pulled onstage. You'll be prodded towards transparency, clarity, and self-disclosure in your own journey towards a strong finish.

It's here in the pointed questions, the reflective, evocative thoughts, that you'll find God's faithful presence urging you onward. It's here that these two mentors invite us to join them in the quest to finish strong and die well.

As a hospital chaplain, as a caregiver to family members, and as a confessed mortality-denier, I know firsthand how vital this quest is. Such directed conversations don't occur naturally in a culture that insists we avoid death-talk as long as possible. Even Christians struggle mightily with addressing this major life issue. We all need that nudge to move beyond "perceived permanence." This book gifts us with that needed nudge.

As we all encounter the three Master Prompters of suffering, relationships, and dying, we will find this book a welcome resource. For self-study, or even better, for small group studies, *Exit Stage Right* is a gem.

Thank you, Lynn and Darrel, for having the discipline to compile this much-needed resource that models faithfulness and transparency.

Virgil Fry
Executive Director, Lifeline Chaplaincy
M. D. Anderson Hospital, Houston, Texas
Author of *Rekindled: Warmed by Fires of Hope* (2007)

CONTENTS

Acknowledgements

This book is a collaborative effort involving more than just the two of us. Key among these are: Dale Ruff and John Elverum who helped develop the concept, and Anne Silkman, Jim Maxwell, Joe Hale, and Joy Dennis, who read the emerging manuscript with careful eyes and loving hearts.

Dr. James Knapp and Dr. Bruce Davis, authors and university professors of gerontology, and Dr. Virgil Fry, Chaplain at M. D. Anderson Hospital, who read the later manuscripts carefully and gave professional council.

Judy Bowyer and Allison Bagley who keyed in countless hours of corrections and chased down endless footnotes.

Our children, Michele Anderson English, Jon Anderson, Tammy Gilbertson Testa, Joe Testa, Kari Gilbertson, Todd Gilbertson, Debbie Anderson Boggs, and Christopher Anderson, who were not bashful about asking pointed questions or advising us to get real.

Hats off also to the consummate professionals at Leafwood Publishers: Dr. Leonard Allen for carefully shepherding this project to completion and Greg Taylor whose editorial wizardry turned our manuscript into a sure-enough book.

Deep thanks especially to our life-long lovers, Barbara Gilbertson and Carolyn Anderson, for their encouragement and patience with this project. They traveled back and forth across Texas with us. They cooked gourmet meals. They provided keen insights and asked powerful questions. They prayed with us and for us. Most of all they have lovingly, passionately shared life and ministry with us for all these rich decades.

Thanks also to a long line of those now deceased who granted us the sacred privilege of walking the last miles of their lives with them and who have thereby mentored us.

Finally, thank you, O Lord God Almighty. You never waste any hurts.

—Darrel Gilbertson and Lynn Anderson

Prologue

"To be grown up is to sit at the table with people who have died, who neither listen nor speak . . ."

—Edna St. Vincent Millay

Glen Davidson inspired the guiding metaphor of this book, "Dying as Theatre."[1] William Shakespeare said, "All the world's a stage." Life is indeed grand theater. And this book borrows the theater metaphor to visit the high drama of finishing strong & dying well.

"The play is the thing." And our title *Exit Stage Right* is itself a little "play on words." The word "exit" means "departure." In this case, departure from the stage of life: the later chapters of life and the final exit—death. The word "right" can mean the direction opposite to "left." But the word "right" also means "correct." So our book is about exiting correctly—the drama of finishing strong & dying well.

We call this drama *"S-aging."* S-aging is a combination of two words: "Sage"—or wisdom. And "aging"—or getting older. Of course, we hardly profess to know the one and only correct way to finish strong & die well. But we do offer our take on the plot of this drama—our experiences in these later scenes—plus our reflections on a healthy exit. And we have both walked the last miles with numerous beloved friends.

We have discovered some clear differences between the way men and women process aging and dying. And those differences raise questions that clearly deserve serious examination. We've shaped our various meetings into a script that plays out like a drama, and so we've restructured a few settings and pieces of dialogue to make it flow better for you as a reader and participant with us in the conversation.

Our little drama here is autobiographical—finishing strong & dying well as explored through the experiences of *two men,* who hardly feel qualified to speak credibly for women. (Our wives have taught us that.)

Of course women are definitely welcomed in the audience, and we hope they will feel included in much of the drama. Yet, our conversations assume that since we are males, the patrons sitting before the stage may be mostly males—thus we will play to men as men. But, after the play, all patrons are invited to the Appendix One for more gender specific information.

So friend, whoever you are we hope you enjoy the play.

"Break a leg."

—Darrel Gilbertson and Lynn Anderson

PLAYERS

Introducing the Actors - Directors

Chapter One

A CAST OF TWO

The two men who both "play the lead roles" as well as "direct the production"

> "All of us are engaged in a life as stage performance, striving to manage the impression others have of us by engaging in an actor/audience agreement throughout life."
>
> — CANADIAN, ERVIN GOFFMAN[1]

KEY QUESTION: We asked ourselves how we might finish our lives strong & die well.

In the 1993 movie, *Grumpy Old Men,* a gang of senior males stumbles around in their own mortality—with outrageous, sometimes irreverent humor as well as poignant insight. But most of the older person characters in that movie are neither *finishing strong* nor *dying well.* A more recent 2008 movie, *The Bucket List,* certainly shows two men finishing strong! But what can *we* do to finish strong & die well?

The script you now hold in your hands is played by two men in the senior season of their lives, who also wrestle with mortality—but who really don't want to go out grumpy. Rather, we want to *finish strong* & *die well*—and help a few others do the same.

Scene 1

Darrel Gilbertson's daughter introduced the authors. She'd lived near Lynn Anderson in Dallas, and one sunny day they stood outside bragging about grandchildren and sharing pastoral "war" stories. Serious health issues had just forced Darrel from ministry sooner than he'd wished. Lynn was transitioning to lead a para-church organization.[2]

Soon after we met we discovered that our lives have followed strikingly parallel pathways. We were within two years of the same age—then at mid sixties. We both grew up in Scandinavian/North American cultural enclaves—both of us were raised on hard work in relatively poor farming operations by seriously religious families. Each of us has been married to his respective wife for more than forty years and both of us have grown children as well as grandchildren.

We have also walked somewhat parallel educational paths. We began in one room country grade schools, then after small high schools filled with hubris and athletic activities, both of us attended private religious colleges. Both earned post graduate degrees in theological studies. And after the age of fifty, both of us pursued Doctor of Ministry degrees.

We have both survived significant cultural relocation, when our ministerial callings uprooted us (Lynn from Western Canada and Darrel from the Upper Midwest) and transplanted us into Texas. Both of us had lengthy tenures as senior ministers of large churches, and we both are somewhat visible within our respective denominations.

More significant to the purposes of this book, for decades both of us have walked closely beside many people who were aging—and dying.

We do acknowledge a pair of differences between us. First, we approach our own mortality from different depth perceptions.

Darrel: I've already outlived medical expectations but see the final grains of sand sliding toward the neck of the hourglass.

Lynn: While keenly aware that the bulk of my sand has drained to the bottom half of his glass, I also assume that, statistically, I may have another decade to live.

Second, theological bents may represent some difference between us as well.

Lynn: My roots are small free church. I'm no fundamentalist, but my theological perspectives may seem somewhat conservative by Darrel's more expansive views.

Darrel: Mine are Lutheran. The trained eye may pick up on some subtle disagreements. If so, we sincerely hope the people in the theater seats profit from these nuances.

However, overall we have come to amazingly convergent emotional and intellectual points in life—albeit by different theological routes. More to the point: we are both aging—and both dying.

In Front of the Old Mill

We draw some lines of our drama from distilled classic literature and scholarly empirical data. But the scenes are mostly played out in front of an old mill.

Darrel: I grew up in a small town in Western Wisconsin, the home of two mills. One mill ground feed for livestock and the other sawed lumber. Both produced "millings." In one sense I see life as a "milling" process. We take the raw materials of our experience; we sort and grind them into more useable forms. So think of this book as some "millings" from the lives of two older souls who, toward the end of the day, want to share what the "long grind" is teaching them.

Lynn: I drove across Croatia in the company of Yale university professor, Miroslov Wolf—who *Christianity Today* magazine named as one of "the five great theologians of the decade."[3] I could hardly believe my good fortune and seized on the opportunity to pick Wolf's magnificent brain. Wolf, however, seemed more interested in wry humor about Croatian political figures than in theological discussion. Finally, Wolf admitted openly, "Actually, I have no interest in *theology,* apart from *ministry.* I have no interest in *ministry* separated from *theology.*" That comment seems now to be more valuable than any answers I might have teased out of him.

In the spirit of Wolf's comment, our millings move between theory and experience, mixing our personal, real-time, street level experiences on growing older and on dying with insights from classic literature and theological reflection on those subjects.

Darrel: I tend to move in an intellectual world of ideas, seeing the big picture, thinking in abstracts.

Lynn: I tend toward more concrete issues, living in a world of experiences, thinking in stories. So as our friendship has grown, I've urged Darrel to share his personal experience with the dying process, believing people would benefit more from those insights than from intellectual theories.

Darrel: Yes, and I keep reminding Lynn that readers may have little interest in my personal experience with mortality and death, apart from a larger framework of writings from major thinkers on these subjects. I've been teaching a course the last few years on "Finishing Strong & Dying Well" in which I combine personal experience with that larger framework—and will do so in this book as well.

Our wish and prayer is that these millings will provide a helpful resource for those on the S-aging journey.

Now you know the ancient cast of two, and having sipped our cognac in front of the old mill, we are ready to raise the curtain on Act One.

Sage Suggestions for a Strong Finish

Key Questions

Complete the following sentences:

1. The first time I needed "bifocals" I remember I felt____________________
____
2. When I go to my doctor for a check up I always wonder if_______________
____
3. My best friend was gravely ill and I wanted to tell him/her______________
____
4. My life altering experience (accident, health issue, or career change) made me assess___________________________________
5. When I first used my AARP Card I felt___________________________
____

Tips for Finishing Strong

How can you talk about your own s-aging?

Some Questions to Ponder

- What might keep you from being taken by surprise by your dying?
- What is the level of awareness and discussion among those closest to you regarding your dying?

Powerline

Since the topic of death and dying is often ignored, neglected, or denied (maybe all three) until it is too late, we decided we needed to talk about it.

Helps

This exercise will help you get started with your life review story:

- Begin a journal of your thoughts. Begin with a brief life story. Then summarize three of the important *events or decisions* that make you who you are.________________________________

  ____
- Continue with three of the most *difficult times* or experiences of your life.____________________________________

  ____
- Conclude this exercise with some critical millings (lessons) life has taught you and how they will apply to your end of life.______________

Chapter Two

BEFORE THE FINAL CURTAIN

"He spent the first years of his marriage accumulating material goods for his family, trying to 'make them a good home,' and by doing so spent most of his time away from home and family. After the occurrence of cancer he spared every moment with them, but by then, it seemed too late."[1]

—ELIZABETH KUBLER-ROSS

KEY QUESTION: How true is the adage "aging is mandatory, but wisdom is optional"?

Scene 2

As Lynn and Darrel moved into life beyond sixty, they found each other to be kindred spirits, both navigating the later years of ministry—and of life. They arranged periodic one and two day conversations—usually either at Darrel's or Lynn's home. They settled into comparing personal soul-journeys into aging generally—and more specifically, toward dying.

Lynn: Darrel, something in me felt drawn to walk beside you as you moved toward dying.

Darrel: I saw you wrestling with the angst of aging and of walking off a familiar life-map into the unmarked frontiers of a new freelance ministry. Of course

I was also delighted to find an experienced comrade in you, Lynn—a soul brother willing to walk beside me to whatever my end might be.

Lynn: Both of us gradually became comfortable talking about Darrel's death, and Darrel introduced me to volumes of "S-aging literature," beginning with Mitch Albom's *Tuesdays with Morrie*,[2] conversations between a professor dying with ALS (Lou Gehrig's disease) and a former-student-become-journalist. At some point Darrel said off-handedly, "Hey, one day we should write a book." I agreed.

We both envisioned recording our conversations in some way similar to *Tuesdays with Morrie*. However a broader horizon began to emerge—a focus on *finishing strong* as well as *dying well.*

Darrel: I guess we assumed that, with age, we might actually become sages of sorts. Which in itself may, admittedly, be a vain senile delusion!

Flashback

Darrel's father died in 1993 and his brother died in 2001—less than ten years apart. Still grieving the death of his father and seeking to reconcile with his brother, Darrel went to see him in Eastern North Carolina. His brother asked him to leave. It was a sad and disappointing end to what had been a sibling friendship—almost Huckleberry Finn-like—as Darrel considered his brother his boyhood hero. That year, Darrel's brother died.

Darrel: My father and brother both died in the same decade. My father's death was not heroic, but it was admirable. I would call him a "poster boy for a good death," even though there were months of morphine for the pain of spinal cancer.

One memory snapshot was the day after Christmas just four months before he died. Dad was put out with God because He had not taken him home. It was on his dying wish list to go on a Christian Holy Day. Usually holiday deaths make the anniversary conflicted—joy and sorrow mixed for the family. But my father's mad-at-God was curiously affirming to me; first because he was okay with his death and, second, he saw a special homecoming aspect to his death.

My father lived and died with a fundamental conviction that his life had meaning—a basic sense of a principle-derived life. Obviously, this means dying is not an isolated event. If we are to *die well,* we first will have to *finish strong.*

My brother's death was like my father's, in that it was also very painful. But by contrast my brother's was a bad death. Toward the end, he grew increasingly withdrawn—from the world, from me, and his family.

Erik Erikson, one of the fathers of modern psychology, says that a common negative ingredient for many in the latter stage of life is despair.[3] That describes my brother—he withdrew. He also grew bitter. One of my death goals is to die like my father rather than my brother.

Lynn: Bingo, another thing we have in common: I too want to die like my Dad. He also died well. Though he suffered enormously, right up until his very painful final days, Dad laughed a lot, loved a good joke or an old story. Even sang a lot. And Dad had zero fear of dying.

By contrast, my friend, Frank died around the same time as Dad, but he died very differently. Frank was hardly sixty years old, but he looked easily a decade older. He was sick, alone, and unemployed. He was a dear friend—but somewhere, years ago, he lost his way. Once during his final months as we lingered over lunch (in a rare moment of self-disclosure) Frank slammed his fist on the table and bellowed, "Lynn, I'm bankrupt." Then punctuating his declaration with some choice expletives, he catalogued his fear and helplessness: "I'm bankrupt financially. Bankrupt physically. I'm bankrupt morally and emotionally. And I guess I'm also bankrupt spiritually, whatever that is. But I don't want to do like so many old codgers do when they get sick and scared—turn to religion. That's a crock of . . ."

Frank went out frightened, pounding his fist on the table. By contrast, Darrel, you and I both want to make our way toward the exit like our fathers did.

But how do we draw the audience into this drama with us?

Darrel: Right, when I tell my friends about our book project, I get a variety of responses, ranging from appreciation to scoffing. Some feared I was "going morbid." This was puzzling to me at first. Even a professional counselor dismissively declared, "For every case of personal angst about one's death, I can show you a hundred cases of indifference." (I am not sure that he could back that up, but it caught me off guard.) At any rate, these varied reactions made me re-visit my motivations. Admittedly I was anxious, but I concluded that the true issue was a layer below anxiety. This one was at the core of my being.

So I have appreciated your consistent encouragement, my friend. Without your support I would not have continued.

Lynn: Well, Darrel, you and I have both seen plenty of *angst* among people facing mortality. Sometimes what looked like *indifference* might have actually been *denial.* A little couplet touches this denial discomfort: "The grief of others, like a pall hangs over all our heads as well, we go there, but are half afraid of him on whom the thunder fell." (author unknown)

Denial of Death seems to be a universal human experience, not merely the title of Ernest Becker's classic book. [4] I am not a mental health professional, but I would question whether indifference to one's mortality is either normal or healthy. That apparent absence of angst may be a clue to the way we in the western world cling desperately to the surface to avoid deeper painful and frightening issues. Consequently, a lot of people face their mortality in quiet desperation and acute loneliness—and in so doing miss some of life's richest texture.

Darrel, you seem unafraid to explore your *core humanity,* even though so many ingredients of modern American life (speed, size, variety, competitiveness) tend to suppress our inner persons. I can't help but believe that your courageous, open approach to dying is very healthy.

Darrel: Yes, at first the resistance of some friends gave me second thoughts. But feedback from classes I am teaching in my active retirement community on "Finishing Strong & Dying Well" definitely confirms that it is not only healthy for me personally to openly process my dying, but that there is a lot of interest out there as well. And hopefully my experience may help some others.

I keep asking myself: Realistically, who wants to think about dying? Who needs to study how to finish life? Who really? And I find myself answering resoundingly: No person living dare shrink from this task. While no two persons experience life exactly alike, all face two things in common: aging and dying.

Lynn: Looks as if we both feel strongly that *silence about our mortality is worse than talking*—and that it is worth writing about it as well.

Darrel: Absolutely. While Thoreau said, "We all live lives of quiet desperation," I don't believe quiet desperation is inevitable. I certainly don't want to go there. I have seen enough of it first hand.

Sage Suggestions for a Strong Finish

Tips for Finishing Strong

- What do you think about the adage, "aging is mandatory, but wisdom optional?" Why do you think that?
- Describe someone close to you that died a "good death" and one who died a "bad death."
- Name a soul mate with whom you might discuss the most vital of all issues—how to finish life? If you do not have such a soul mate, how might you find one?

Power Line

- Since talking about our mortality is important and time sensitive, we must get past initial fears and procrastination by the age of fifty.

Helps

This is a reading exercise we suggest you use for study and reflection:

- Find a copy of the Holy Bible and look up Ecclesiastes. Or try an internet search. This is a "post-modern" author with high levels of skepticism and big doses of realism regarding life. Page through the book to get an overview.

- Now read *Ecclesiastes* in one sitting and then ask what the "Philosopher Sage"—best translation of the title—said to you (first impressions will likely be more important than your studied conclusions).
- In what ways do you share the point of view of *Ecclesiastes* and in what ways do you not? (This may be the beginning of your search for a lasting or final wisdom).

Chapter Three

THE DANGERS OF DENIAL

"In this country, some people start being miserable about growing old while they are still young."

—MARGARET MEAD AN AMERICAN ANTHROPOLOGIST

"Dying is a very dull, dreary affair. And my advice to you is to have nothing whatever to do with it."

—W. SOMERSET MAUGHAM

KEY QUESTION: How do we break through our defenses of denial?

Scene 3

The conversations take a turn toward living with a terminal illness and dying. Darrel is an early riser, and this morning Lynn finds Darrel sitting on the back porch, his hands around a cup of coffee. Darrel takes a sip from his coffee, leans forward with his elbows on the table and welcomes his friend to a bright new Texas morning.

Darrel: Sometimes humor helps us confront death. T. S. Eliot said that "humor is also a way of saying something very serious." Laughter eases our awkwardness, helps us approach issues that are so big we don't know how to talk about them directly. This past winter I taught a course for senior male adults on "Finishing Strong & Dying Well." And I jokingly outlined the course: One for the money, two for the show, three to get ready, and four to go! Maybe a clumsy attempt at humor—but humor, like art, comes in below the radar and catches people off guard, inviting an openness to rethink the unthinkable.

Lynn: My brother-in-law is a master at this. He is in his late seventies, had recent surgeries (bypass and hip replacement), but his humorous metaphor for dying is “tipping over,” as in “I heard that ol’ Pete tipped over.” When I called him after his surgery he quipped, “Well so far, I’m still *on top of the grass*. Haven’t tipped over yet.”

Darrel: Yes, humor can help. But of course death is no laughing matter. Psychologists call facing our death the primary human issue.

Death Thought and Denial

Darrel: We are never very far from thoughts of death. Yet, people seem to be unprepared to face this most important part of our existence. At least a number of intellectual heavyweights seem to agree. Soren Kierkegaard, [1] a couple of decades before Sigmund Freud, and many scholars since have understood that the core problem of our humanity is our dying. Yet it is the psychologically unthinkable. Freud even called our common denial response the “vital lie,” by which he meant that denial is a necessary illusion. He felt that most of us must deny death thoughts because we are not sure we can deal with the horror of our own oblivion.

Lynn: The death-thought lurks in our shadows. It haunts our dreams and hovers over our conversations. Disturbs our internal peace. Harry Emerson Fosdick said, “The reason we make so much noise on New Year’s Eve is to drown out the macabre sound of grass growing on our own graves.” That sound could be likened to a key on one instrument in an orchestra, stuck down on a shrill note. It doesn’t bother us too much while the full orchestra is playing. But as the instruments die away one by one, that shrill note screams louder and louder until it fills the whole sky.

Darrel: Ernest Becker’s *The Denial of Death* tutored me as I prepared for my S-aging classes. Becker wrote this book in 1973 but it still connects solidly with today’s culture. He insists that frankly facing our death is “the beginning of wholeness." [2] And this wholeness helps us finish strong. Facing our mortality teaches us many highly important lessons—whereas denial stuffs down or represses these lessons.

Help From Great Thinkers

Lynn: Help me understand Freud and Becker: Did Freud's "vital lie" suggest that lying to oneself about one's own death is healthy?

Darrel: Sigmund Freud extended Darwin's survival of species theory to develop his psychoanalysis therapy. For Freud "the vital lie" was not a "moral slip." The *vital* in vital lie regarded denial of death as the key to the survival of the species. Freud linked *eros* and *thanatos* (sexuality and death). Sexual climax is a little death—one of many examples—which is a foreshadowing of my big death.

Becker argues, however, that Freud took the idea too far. And I agree with Becker. Becker summarized his criticism of Freud with the words of Otto Rank (a former student and devotee of Freud, but later a critic): "Man is a *theological* being, and not merely a *biological* one." [3] In other words, biology is an incomplete explanation of human nature.

Acknowledging little deaths as part of the processes of dying goes beyond biology to the root meaning of our existence. Again, I see this as "the *very core of my own soul.*" Which is why Becker's contribution is so important.

Romantic Implications

Darrel: To be more personal: to dissect my love for Barbara in the biological model alone—only hormones and sex drive—would be a very impoverished and sorry view of love. After fifty years as best friends, steady daters, and then decades of married life, she still lights up my room. This luminosity has no neat or simple reductivity such as Freud might ascribe to it. Rather it is multi-nuanced with layers of conscious memories as well as unconscious emotions—and larger than any life story. Dare I insist that this kind of love is theological, not just biological? God has poured out his love into our hearts by the Holy Spirit, whom he has given us.[4]

Love—and life and death—are all much larger than biology.

Freud and Anderson

Lynn: Yes! Freud's kind of love doesn't run deep enough. Genuine love—like death and life—is metaphysical, even spiritual, and far more profound than anyone's reductionist theories. It burns even more brightly in the seasons of life when the sex drive barely flickers. Of course this spiritual dimension applies to all the larger elements of our core humanity—not the least of which is death.

Remember Frank? He pounded his fists on the table then went out frightened. Could this have been something of what the Philosopher Sage of Ecclesiastes had in mind?

> Remember your Creator
> in the days of your youth,
> before the days of trouble come
> and the years approach when you will say,
> "I find no pleasure in them"—
> before the sun and the light
> and the moon and the stars grow dark,
> and the clouds return after the rain;
> when the keepers of the house tremble,
> and the strong men stoop,
> when the grinders cease because they are few,
> and those looking through the windows grow dim;
> when the doors to the street are closed
> and the sound of grinding fades;
> when men rise up at the sound of birds,
> but all their songs grow faint;
> when men are afraid of heights
> and of dangers in the streets;
> when the almond tree blossoms
> and the grasshopper drags himself along
> and desire no longer is stirred.
> Then man goes to his eternal home
> and mourners go about the streets.[5]

Darrel: Yes, what is true in love is also true in death. I hope my flurry of big words doesn't get in the way of my true feelings.

Sigmund, Ernest, and Darrel

Lynn: Some big words and lofty ideas indeed. And oh, so helpful! However, I doubt the average S-aging or dying person will be contemplating his or her own demise in such abstract concepts. Can you help me connect this with your own street level life experiences?

Darrel: Okay, Lynn. Let me descend from the clouds to a very personal level. My take is this: if my vision of dying was *only revealed as only physical*, per Freud, I might miss the obvious. All of my life experience now witnesses to its end, pushing me to accept the inevitable. Little deaths multiply and I see the handwriting on the wall.

- My body aches and throbs with viruses and allergies that never before bothered me,
- "Vanities of vanities" abound as I try to climb ladders, miss my nap, map out too big a day schedule, and pretend I am still forty years old.
- I lose spiritual altitude when I bitterly rant at the world's wickedness, succumbing to the siren's call of complaint and lament.

Yet the very acceptance of my death is marvelously freeing. On the opposite pole from Freud, facing my mortality is a *vitalizing truth* rather than a *vital lie*.

Lynn: Darrel, what you have been saying really rings bells. My life—what is left of it—is beginning to look very different to me than at any time before. I too am seeing many things as little deaths, even my stiff joints—and my slower jogging. Fact is, Darrel, at our age if it ain't hurtin', it ain't workin'.

But this sense of mortality doesn't just show up in our final years. To some degree it dogs our steps all our adult lives. And I hear you say that our consciousness of mortality keeps changing shape with the changing stages of life. What sort of developmental timeline might we expect our growing mortality consciousness to follow?

Evil Twins

Darrel: Of course, timelines are general, but in my own experience the death thought begins gradually replacing the indestructibility thoughts from forty or fifty years of age on. And how we deal with this really matters. Evil twins of *denial* and *withdrawal* that lurk during S-aging can really take us down.

Lynn: Tell me about the evil twins.

Darrel: Evil Twin number one is *denial*. Denial is the primary (Alpha Twin) evil of bad aging—and it is also our most common blind spot (an illusion that we shall live forever). It is the Prime Sin—"you shall be like God," the Seducer offered Adam in the Garden of Eden. Until we grasp the reality of our death we will struggle both *heroically* and *tragically*. We *heroically* struggle to stay young, swallow the big lie of our immortality, vainly preen and camouflage. We *tragically* try to defeat death, which can lead, as Martin Luther suggests, to the final great and terrible sin of despair.

Lynn: Words from another ancient Hebrew poet come to mind here: "Teach us to number our days aright that we may gain a heart of wisdom."[6]

And the second Evil Twin, Darrel?

Darrel: Evil Twin number two is *withdrawal*. It is the secondary (Beta Twin) and is the outflow of denial. It is a fraternal though not identical twin. People burnout and brownout in careers, marriages, and in faith/spirituality when they cling to their worship of lost youth. But if we can accept lost youth as a personal reality, then we can mature step by step, (S-age) in wisdom, wellness, and wholeness of body and soul. I continue battling daily, because my temptation is to give up the fight and surrender to the Evil Twins.

Shattered Invincibilty

Darrel: Even at age 64 I felt somewhat invincible—until a life-threatening diagnosis abruptly forced me to be profoundly conscious of my own limitations. At 57 I took a parish in a hyper-ambitious suburb, mostly college graduates, notorious for both financial success and troubled lives. Ah, here I could finish my career with sizzle.

However, the first two years turned out to be pretty awful. Resistance to change. Bare bones staff, killer work loads (literally killer for me) and impossible expectations in the pew. I was miserable.

But eventually tensions dialed back. Finances improved, staff grew. So did results. I suppose because I had weathered the storm, I began to feel invincible again.

But then came excessive fatigue. Reflux. Short breath. Digestive track disturbance (aggressive colitis). Then several surgeries—leading to discovery of my fatal disease! I recall one Sunday riding past the church en route to the hospital ER, inwardly raging at my helplessness.

Sorting through all this was mellowing me out, surprising even to myself, when the ultimate blow fell. Yet the dark news of my fast-track-death-trajectory did not throw me into depression or shock. In fact, I thought *so-this-is-the-hand-I-am-dealt* and basically took it in stride.

Lynn: I'm curious—classic literature suggests that our sense of mortality unfolds in some predictable sequence of *Life Stages*. How much of your matter-of-factness is age of life related—thus somewhat predictable for most people at your age? And how much is unique to your personal wiring? Or how much flows from your personal faith?

Darrel's Journey

Darrel waits a while to answer, as if organizing something in his mind.

Darrel: You asked me that some months ago. I didn't answer directly then, but I will try now: Yes, I do believe people will respond differently at various life-stages. And, of course, wiring is a variable as well. But frankly, I want to believe that, for me, much of it is the latter—faith related. For me there is no avoiding God.

Remember when I told you about returning to my boyhood family church for my mother's funeral and seeing an old familiar picture on the wall behind the altar? I was stunned because I had not seen that picture in fifty years. As a child in worship, I would sit for hours (bored to tears) gazing up at the lovely picture of Jesus the Good Shepherd on a lonely path, carrying home a lost lamb slung over his shoulders. I described that image to you as the basic template of my faith—a searching and loving God. And I think the image of God's favoring face is what keeps me relatively calm in these years since my diagnosis.

But that is only part of the story. To be honest, Lynn, your question has also pointed my journey in some new directions. I have become more convinced that the seasons of life also come powerfully into play.

STAGES—WIRING—FAITH

Flipping through his notes, Darrel pulls out a sheet and turns it so Lynn can see it with him.

Darrel: Let me show you how developmental psychologist Erik Erikson framed this journey. This piece has been very helpful to me in sorting through my life experience.

Darrel began reading the chart aloud while both men swapped comments:

Stages and Issues of Life

Stage One—Oral-Sensory	Trust vs. Mistrust
Stage Two—Muscular-Anal	Autonomy vs. Shame/Doubt
Stage Three—Locomotor	Initiative vs. Guilt
Stage Four—Latency	Industry vs. Inferiority
Stage Five—12-18 years	Identity vs. Role Confusion
Stage Six—19-40 years	Intimacy vs. Isolation
Stage Seven—40-65 years	Generativity vs. Stagnation
Stage Eight—Maturity	Ego Integrity vs. Despair
Stage Nine—Elderhood	Gerotranscendance vs. Withdrawal

Darrel: Stage Nine was added posthumously by Joan Erikson.[7] I, not the Eriksons, added the words "Elderhood" and "Withdrawal."

For example at age 40 I suspect I may have reacted quite differently to my diagnosis. Now I track the seasons of life with a larger appreciation for the *enlarged* community-wide scope of my seasons (Levinson)[8] rather than *narrower* mere individual development (Erikson). Life is not just interpersonal. Rather, it is *transpersonal*. And of course, as Erikson's schematic explains, life is continuously evolving. We keep changing as long as we live.

Thanks for the observation and help, my friend!

Lynn gives Darrel a high five.

Lynn: You keep stretching my thinking too, Darrel—you are nudging me toward my own more reflective life-season. You are also helping me feel increasingly more conscious of, and yet less morbid about, my own inevitable death as well.

Darrel: I think this is a major step forward for you, friend. Because we definitely are both terminal.

Lynn: Definitely. Willie Nelson sings it this way:

What will you do with the sands of time,
When they carve out lines around your eyes?
I can clench my fist just as tight as I can,
But I can't hold back the sands of time. [9]

I hear you, Willie. Hear you too, Darrel. And I, too, plan to finish strong & die well. However, I am still looking at mortality from a more detached perspective than you. But I do want to see it better.

Silent reflective moments pass; Lynn releases his breath slowly.

Lynn: Where do we go from here?

End of Scene Three

Sage Suggestions for a Strong Finish

Tips for Finishing Strong

- *Remember* there are good deaths and bad deaths. Both. Silence about our dying is worse than talking, so talk about how you felt at the most recent funeral you attended.
- *Know* that the proper age to deal with death is always the one we are living at the time. So talk about the first person whose death you recall.
- *Find* today's obituary section of your local paper and read it. Now: What thoughts and feelings come to mind?

Powerline

We discovered a cultural conspiracy of silence on the topic and set ourselves the task to read what learned people have said about dying and death.

Helps

To sharpen your awareness and help expose denial or its variant forms try these questions:

- How would you experience the difference between the Evil Twins *Denial* and *Withdrawal*?
- Describe the first time you remember catching a glimpse of your own death (or faced the hard truth of your own death?)
- Ask yourself these further questions:
  - a. How have I lived in response to that awakening to my mortality?
  - b. How open or honest have I been with myself?
  - c. Who do you talk with or speak to about your fears, hopes and plans?
- Start a journal (Lynn and Darrel both journal; Darrel has two) as a breakthrough from the silence.

SETTING THE STAGE

Three Backdrops for the Drama of S-aging

Chapter Four

SET ONE: THE PATHWAY OF AGES AND STAGES

"All right, I can see the broken eggs. Where's this omelette of yours?" [1]

—PANAIT ISTRATI ON THE FAILURES OF COMMUNISM IN THE USSR

KEY QUESTION: How do I avoid being narrow or myopic in my own view of the life I lead?

Scene 4

It is six A.M. in San Antonio, Texas, and the sun is rising over the hill country as Darrel and Lynn sit quietly sipping coffee. Months have passed since their last face-time visit. After some social catching up they fall silent—searching for the place to pick up their S-aging conversation again. Eventually, Darrel breaks the silence.

Darrel: Life is indeed grand theater—the curtain is rising on yet another day. Life plays out on our stage, one scene at a time. So let's choose the back drops for the main acts in our S-aging drama.

This comment triggered a whole morning's lively discussion during which we hammered out three stage sets:

- The pathway of ages and stages
- The card game of circumstances
- The trap door of perceived permanence

Omelets are Messy

Lynn: Darrel, the other day you e-mailed me this Istrati quote about broken eggs without an omelet. [See the epigram at the beginning of this chapter] Where does this fit in our conversations about finishing strong & dying well?

Darrel: Indeed I did. For me, that famous Istrati quote means that the life transitions from about forty-five years of age to the end of life involve breaking a few eggs. That is, to S-age well, some fairly radical shifts are required in the last half of life, shifts that run a lot deeper than surface things like dropping contact sports and beefing up our 401K. Rather, these shifts happen down at the psycho-social level. They actually constitute a sort of soul displacement.

In Flannery O'Connor's short story, "The Displaced Person," a strong willed, Protestant, southern, female landowner seeks a farmhand. At first she had consented to hiring a World War II refugee, but then changed her mind. "Mr. Guizac is not satisfactory," she said. "He *doesn't fit in*. I have to have somebody who fits in."[2]

Having worked with hundreds of refugees, we would not minimize the geographical and cultural changes they face as they seek to "fit in." During *life transitions* in which we are morphing into another emergent self or identity, the displacement struggle to re-fit may arguably be as disorienting as the cultural shock a refugee experiences. At some of these times between stages in life we do not appear to know ourselves. We may feel our eggs being smashed but not yet see an omelet cooking.

My Wife's Several Husbands

Lynn: Gotcha! Darrel, this morphing reminds me that my wife Carolyn says she has been married to at least five different men over the last fifty years—and all five of them are named Lynn Anderson! But Darrel, what are some eggs that get smashed along the way?

Darrel: To answer that question, let me show you the big screen for this part of the S-aging drama with *The Pathway of Ages and Stages.* I don't want to drift off into abstractions here, so look over my shoulder at this graphic I've cobbled together from several sources[3]:

Life's Four Acts (or Scenes)

Scene One	Scene Two
The First *Age* of life from one to twenty-five. Here we meet multiple basic issues—trust, ego-formation, differentiation from parents, etc. In short, we are shaping our identity and character.	The Second Age roughly from twenty-five to fifty takes us into further identity evolvement, and, through what Erik Erikson dubbed the "midlife crisis." Here we also confront heavy duty life-meaning issues—including mortality. I'm inclined to agree with those who say that "all questions after thirty-five are questions about our dying!"
Scene Three	**The Final Scenes**
The Third Age is our focus in this book. Some call it "pre-retirement" which begins somewhere between fifty to seventy years of age, and continues into the Fourth Age. In his excellent book *Halftime*,[4] Bob Buford calls this the shift of focus "from success to significance." During this Age, the heavier mortality issues move to center stage. (Or—in the case of denial artists—get driven deeper into the wings.)	The Fourth Age (roughly seventy years and up)—plays out more of an existential drama with the mortality issues, but usually in a more mellow and in a matter of fact way. Here the more practical and physical dimensions of aging and dying—and putting ones house in order—take center stage.

Years ago, Peggy Lee sang it for us: "Is that all there is?"[5] Her song touched the point in life when we find at least one broken egg—and start wondering "is this all there is to life?" The strategies and results of the first half of life begin to lose flavor and, as they did for The Philosopher Sage in Ecclesiastes, they take on the character of a burden or a curse. Eggs are definitely breaking—but we are seeing no omelet! At this point in life, we begin to sense we are on a pathway but we don't see a destination.

However, three major life issues begin to awaken on both the conscious and the unconscious levels:

1. Who am I?
2. Why do I die?
3. What has been my contribution?

Of course, these can be repressed for a time, but not forever. And repression will usually distort our core perception of life itself.

The Winning of Success

All along the Pathway of Ages and Stages, we are growing a new identity (more accurately, a series of new identities), formulating our legacy, and wrestling with our finitude. For example, every purchase of a life insurance policy is a roll of the dice of mortality.

And then the Fourth Age is the time when we begin to make an omelet out of the broken eggs. No wonder we feel out of place! My omelet quote points to the scrambled confusion we experience before we move on and begin to transform the egg of our former self from a pursuer of *success* to the omelet of a discoverer of *significance*.

Lynn: The picture is getting clearer. But you have left it in general and not yet specific terms. So, here comes my old probing question again: Where is Darrel? How have you or are you personally experiencing these ages? What did some of your broken eggs look like as these various stages surfaced out of place feelings in you personally?

The curtain closes with Lynn's question hanging in the air. Before the next scene opens, ponder the question for yourself.

Sage Suggestions for a Strong Finish

Remember how it shocked Tom Brokaw when he discovered in his interviews for his book, *The Greatest Generation,* that many (if not most) World War II veterans did not tell their stories because they thought no one would find them interesting? Is your personal story special? The answer is "Of course, because of your broken eggs and omelets."

Helps

To acknowledge how strange truth really is in your life, try this exercise:

- Tell about one of your broken eggs.
- Tell a story from your life when the very worst thing that could happen did happen. But in the long view of life, it worked out fine.
- Tell about a time when you thought something was the greatest, but then in the long run worked out badly.
- Draw at least one conclusion about this strange truth of your life ______ ______________(this might be the start of the recipe for your omelet).

Powerline

It is not necessary (or good) to wait for inspiration to tell or write about your life—just start talking and/or writing, thus giving wings to your words (and omelet to your eggs).

Helps

- Your greatest life lesson tool is the power of personal narrative, your Story):
- Your Story is a combination of autobiography and lessons. It is one-of-a-kind. How do you feel about the possibility it could be lost or forgotten?
- Start simply: do not over-analyze.
- Review your story in the light of the observations in this chapter and then re-write or revise your thoughts. Think hard.

Chapter Five

SET TWO: THE CARD GAME OF CIRCUMSTANCE

On turning 70—"You still chase women, but only downhill."

On turning 80—"That is the time of your life when even your Birthday Suit needs pressing."

On turning 90—"You know you're getting old when the candles cost more than the cake."

—Bob Hope

"You know you are getting old when everything either dries up or leaks."

—Will Rogers

KEY QUESTION: In what ways do the cards dealt by circumstances interact with life Ages and Stages in the S-aging drama?

Scene 5

Lynn had come to hear Darrel preach at Resurrection Lutheran Church in Plano, Texas. By this time, preaching was becoming very difficult for Darrel. They talked as they spent the day together, before and after the assembly, at lunch, in the car, and back at the house.

Lynn: Darrel, your explanation of *Life's Four Ages and Stages* significantly helps set the stage on which we play out the S-aging drama. I am really with you there.

However, may I suggest an additional stage-set for S-aging? Besides living out the S-aging drama along the *Pathway of Ages and Stages* I think we also play out the drama against a backdrop I call *The Card Game of Circumstance.* In my mind, this stage set does not replace the natural and sequential *Pathway of Ages and Stages,* but overlays it and may sometimes modify its impact and even its sequence. As I see it, circumstances cannot be completely separated from the developmental sequence. However, *Ages and Stages* follow in a predictable sequence, like a pathway, while circumstances fall upon us randomly, like the hand we are dealt in a game of cards.

For example: you and I are both in our late sixties, at a similar mile-marker along the developmental pathways of *Ages and Stages*—and thus predictably expect similar broken eggs at our point on the journey. But, circumstance has randomly dealt you a different hand of cards than it has dealt me. Our circumstances are significantly different, even though our life-paths are parallel. To put it bluntly, you have been diagnosed with a fatal disease. I have not. So try as I might, I cannot perceive and process life's big issues in the same way or at the same level of urgency as you—in spite of the similarity in our ages.

Darrel Smells a Cop-Out

Darrel: Lynn, I'm still not sure you get my point. I'm wondering if (in spite of noble intentions) you are still into a measure of a busyness and time-prioritizing schedule syndrome—like what distracted Martha who stirred around resentfully in the kitchen while her sister Mary sat at Jesus' feet (Luke 10:38-42). If so, that set does not fit on the same stage with my backdrop. But it isn't just you I am thinking about, my friend. So many people appear to be running in circles instead of straightening their line to a destination and slowing the pace to last for the long haul—and to enjoy the journey.

While we mortals find a lot of ways to deny our mortality, I am convinced that *busy-ness* is the most common denial mechanism.

But then, of course, old pastors tend to get grumpy and judgmental—even Lutheran ones. And this is a free country so you do have a right to defend yourself. Sorry for the blindside, but I'll bet I have your full attention!

Darrel grins with his disarming waggle of the eyebrows. Lynn stares back, a long pause, struggling to dismiss feelings of defensiveness in favor of introspection. Finally he responds, a bit tentatively.

Lynn: Wow! That is definitely something for me—and a world full of busy people—to chew on, since a person obviously could attempt to repress his or her aging and mortality issues by staying busy. We can certainly be out of touch with our own stuff.

I may have to plead guilty to the busy accusation. But I am not necessarily ready to plead guilty to all of the rest of those charges—especially the vanity denial ones. Rather, Darrel, I think you are actually confirming my point: Your response sounds to me like a clear example of our difference in perception due to the difference in *circumstances*—we are not holding the same cards.

Darrel: Fair enough. But you will need to help me because on the surface you sound as if you see my life becoming a study in minimalism—and that would actually promote the very age-ist bias our S-aging drama protests. Finishing strong means a rich menu of activities from which to choose daily—not shriveling into minimalism.

Hundreds of people in my active adult community (most in the Fourth Age) will tell you that their lives are hardly narrow and restricted.

Honey, I Won't Shrink the Older Kids!

Lynn: No question that humankind is prone to invent all sorts of mechanisms to mask the denial of their mortality. But even during retirement, some people stay stuck on busy. Some even while they are dying, hurry around, busy at less than significant activities and projects—to the neglect of some significant priorities. Yes, *busyness* may well be the most common of denial mechanisms. However, I am still not fully convinced that my many projects make me your poster boy for vanity denial.

In my *Card Game of Circumstance* I am definitely not thinking minimalism or age bias. Just the opposite, in fact. Let me illustrate further: again, while you and I are in a similar *Age* or *Life Stage*, Darrel, our *Circumstances* are quite different, and this impacts our S-aging process. I am still healthy and still in career mode—thus I perceive myself (rightly or wrongly) as having enough time and energy to squander some of it on a few relatively meaningless activities that I find enjoyable—while still not neglecting the truly significant top priorities. You hold a different hand from mine. And a person with my cards can't fully understand how you should play yours—and vice versa.

Holding Different Cards

Lynn: But Darrel, the fact that you have been pushed into retirement not by age, but by illness does not at all suggest that you have resigned from usefulness nor would you quit important activities. Quite the contrary. It means you now have both the opportunity and the perspective to focus on activities that are the most useful and important.

Forced retirement is one card that circumstance has randomly dealt you—but it is a card I don't hold. Someone has defined retirement as getting to do all the time what matters most to you. Retirement usually allows a person the discretionary time to run deeper and to zero in on the central, most significant issues. Darrel, you have stepped out of the many projects phase of your life, not in order to shrivel toward *minimalism,* but to zero in on what is of *maximum importance* to you. That is one way your circumstances and mine differ. In fact, in my circumstances I have a difficult time seeing what is of maximum importance as clearly as you. And while I can intellectually acknowledge my own mortality, it would be unfair to expect me—or anyone who is not in your circumstance—to discern priorities as clearly as you can discern yours or to feel what you feel.

However, more importantly, you hold another card I don't have in my hand: *Circumstance* has dealt you the Ace of Spades—the diagnosis of a fatal disease. You are hyper-aware that your time is limited, and you daily experience diminishing energy. But the upside is that terminal illness has sharpened your priorities to a short list of those things of greatest significance. For example, one of your top priorities is *this book.* It is also a priority for me, but only one among many.

At the same time, in spite of all the downsides that go with a terminal diagnosis, you relish more richly some valuable life ingredients that you might otherwise have more or less taken for granted. And your circumstances lead you to savor each day of life with an intensity that one in my health circumstances can't fully fathom. I see you so obviously choosing to live out what Abraham Lincoln said: "In the end, it's not the years in your life that count. It's the life in your years."

These things are in the cards for you. But (so far as I know at least) a fatal diagnosis is not in the cards for me. So you and I are sitting at the table, playing out the same game but holding different hands of cards. In terms of S-aging, you hold a handful of aces, while I am still holding my low cards with only limited perception of how the hand will play out—or when.

Also, because of the cards I am holding (these differing circumstances), what I perceive as normal late career activity for me might appear from the perspective of one holding your cards to be mere superficial busyness (vanity denial). All the while, as you have well said of course, both of us feel a gravitational force trying to tug us backward into denial, withdrawal—or even bitterness or despair.

Splendid Maximalism

Lynn: My friend, far from seeing your life as a study in minimalism, I see you as the poster boy for maximalism. And frankly, in a strange sort of way, I feel a bit envious. Though circumstances have limited your time and energy, you steadfastly refuse to give in to gravitational pull. Rather, from among the rich range of activities before you, you have deliberately chosen to pursue the few most significant ones. Splendid maximalism. You refuse to fold 'em till your last card is played. Hats off to you, my friend.

What is more, I get spill-over benefits from your experience. You are helping me (and many others) to begin working through the implications of getting older: the real meaning of life and the looming reality of my own death time. And, like you, I don't plan to stop living until I am dead. I can't thank you enough for that, my fellow S-aging pilgrim.

Darrel: Honestly, I may have been projecting my own history on you—pressing you to play your hand with my cards. And I may even be equating finishing strong with having a rich menu of activities from which to choose. Fair enough. Maybe.

I would argue, however, that vanity denial is a layer deeper than the psychological and on the same level as the theological dimension of denial. Kubler-Ross identified bargaining as an intermediary grief stage in grieving over one's own dying. Vanity denial is bargaining—pretense on steroids.

The writer of the Old Testament book of Ecclesiastes (best translated Philosopher-Sage) awakened me to my own failed and silly self-justifications. For example, I looked for comfort in the actuarial hedge on my life expectancy after diagnosis of PSC. (According to the best estimate of life expectancy, I still could have six years to live! I carefully calibrated.) That was my vanity denial—my slick-looking and cleverly devised attempt to postpone facing up to my certain death.

A Small White Flag

Lynn: Looks like we mortals are all occasionally susceptible to some forms of self-delusion. Thanks for the prodding. The possibility of vanity denial is something I definitely need to think seriously about. Presumably, most people who are in denial, *deny* they are in denial! You definitely have me looking under emotional rocks. I hope some folks out there in our audience will want to do the same.

I certainly must admit that for much of my life I assumed that my over-commitment was normal. Across time the furious pace had become a way of life. But as I get older my body begins to balk and I feel hampered by it—even angry at the thing for its lack of cooperation. However, with your coaching I am coming to accept that it is okay to move toward a pace of living that is more nearly normal for a person my age. What is more, I would have become convinced that this adjustment is actually a part of finishing strong. Thanks for steering me toward a more mellowed, reflective, and relationship-rich way of life.

Take Your Time

Lynn: The novelist Thomas Wolfe once gushed that he wanted "to ride all the trains, read all the books and sleep in all the beds."[1] I can understand Wolfe's feeling. But you are helping me see that at such a pace, I do not exhaust events; they exhaust me! Vitality consists in *quality* of life, not merely in *quantity*. While I believe that eternal life is life that lasts forever, I also believe that is only a fragment of the story. An eternity of low quality life would be a curse, not a blessing. Actually, the biblical concept of eternal life has more to do with how *well* we live than with how *long*.[2]

Darrel: One thing I see in the cards for you is that specifically and personally—day by day, step by step, going ever more slowly—indeed you are also discovering that less is more.

Lynn: Precisely, my slower-living friend, and that resonates with words from the mouth of St. Francis of Assisi:

> *If you want to live life free,*
> *take your time, go slowly.*
> *Do few things but do them well,*
> *heartfelt joys are holy.*[3]

Darrel: *[grinning]* Yes, I like what Charles Zanor said. Asked if any life changes resulted from his bout with cancer, Zanor answered, "Since my chemotherapy treatment, I have experienced small Zen rushes—an arresting sense of tranquility coupled with the heightened awareness that what I am doing at that moment is exactly what I want to be doing—whether I'm sitting in a restaurant with a newspaper, reading a book in bed, cooking a meal or watching a movie with my wife. Maybe this is just a case of the moment-by-moment living some say is the natural sequela of any protracted battle for health . . . Maybe I need a new philosophy . . . [but] in the meantime, I'll have a Reuben on rye."[4]

So the drama goes on. We play out our versions of S-aging on a split set: partly on The Pathway of Ages—the natural unfolding of life stages; partly in The Card Game of Circumstances—the random happenings that uniquely shape each life. After a brief intermission the curtain will rise on Act III, The Trapdoor of Perceived Permanence.

Sage Suggestions for a Strong Finish

Some people surrender to gravitational pull and become victims of their circumstances. Why? What possibility seems most tempting to you:

- They conclude their circumstances cannot be changed, so trying to escape them is an exercise in futility—rather than a really hard learning opportunity.
- They lack the courage or the will to rise above them.
- They are unaware of the stages of human development and /or don't know what is normal at their stage of life.
- They get lost or swamped in the details and forget the whole story of their life (perspective).
- They do not realize that most opportunities for growth take place through small incremental steps and there are only a few leaps at tall buildings for the average life.
- Other______________________________

Powerline

You may consider it odd but we truly believe that no scrap of human experience is ever wasted when adventurous hope is our beacon in the dark.

Helps

- At what Age or Stage of life development are you?
- What compelling circumstance might be further shaping you right now? What might your circumstances be doing to change you?
- What can you do to change your circumstances?
- If they are unchangeable, what opportunity for positive personal character growth do they provide?
- What first step or next step should you take to deal positively with your circumstances?
- Search websites for a feast of in-depth stuff: try using key words like "aging" or "positive psychology" or even "worry," for examples—you will be surprised at the number of books, essayists and bloggers and their wide rage of interests in these issues.

Chapter Six

SET THREE: THE TRAPDOOR OF PERCEIVED PERMANENCE

"Old friends, old friends,
Sat on their park bench like bookends…
Sharing the same fears."

—Simon and Garfunkel [1]

KEY QUESTION: What issues do you need to face in order to escape the illusion of *perceived permanence*?

Scene 6

Ominous clouds moved overhead and chilling gusts of February wind drive Darrel and Lynn from their balcony perch to the warmth and welcome of Lynn's study. The scene opens as they continue mentally piecing together backdrops for their S-aging drama.

Lynn: Can it be healthy for a person to fret over living too long, Darrel? One of my significant early mentors was an indefatigable pioneer missionary, J.C. Bailey, who passed away at the age of 97. Born in 1903, Bailey made his last trip to India when he was 88 years old. When he was past 95, J.C. received word that a life-long friend, the last of his inner circle of contemporaries, had just died. Bailey wept a few minutes. Then, recovering his composure, proclaimed to his son John:

I feel like one,

Who treads alone,
Some banquet hall deserted.
Whose lights are fled,
Whose garlands dead,
And all but he departed.

This characteristic flight of eloquence meant, in plain terms, "I am dying too late."

Darrel: That sounds healthy to me. The danger of *perceived permanence* is the note that the Philosopher Sage kept sounding throughout the book of Ecclesiastes. Maybe because most of us won't get it the first time around—and he kept giving us yet another nudge. Or as Shapiro puts it, "Uncomfortable with the truth of our own transience, we need to have it pointed out to us over and over again."[2]

Varieties of Camouflage

Darrel: I have identified "busy-ness" as perhaps the most common camouflage hiding the trap-door of *perceived permanence*. However, busyness is only one cover. *Things* can be another. Though most older people have quite limited subsistence income, many have tempting levels of disposable income—which can lead to the illusion of *permanence. Youthfulness* is yet another more obvious way of luring people toward the trap door. For example, *The Wall Street Journal* quoted a dermatologist who was marketing this brand of repression: "A telegenic 55-year-old dermatologist delivered the promise his audience had come to hear: you can have more energy and even reverse the aging process."[3]

Then there is the *diet frenzy*—some of us starve ourselves, not for legitimate health reasons, but to look young in a vain attempt to feed the *perception that we are permanent.*

Lynn: I think Shapiro and Solomon are right. I know I certainly have trouble getting it. Darrel, maybe I might need another nudge.

Something From M*A*S*H

Darrel: Okay, here's the nudge, Lynn: Until a person begins to triage life, they have not fully begun the task of authentic reckoning with their mortality.

Triaging means classifying the severity of the wound. We are old enough to remember the doctors in the 1970s TV series, M*A*S*H. As the wounded are removed from the helicopters, the anguished look on these doctor's faces, in the midst of urgent life and death decisions, frames the core business of the Third Age in which "the heavier mortality issues move to center stage" (see the chart on page 45).

When a person triages life and its future (acknowledges the reality and seriousness of the mortality wound), they can begin to move on from vanity land. But hey, even if we need another nudge, I guess it's nothing to be embarrassed about. Some other very smart people sometimes need help with triage. For example, brilliant theologian Richard John Neuhaus wrote about his near death (he called it "after death") experience as a life epiphany. His *triage moment.*[5] Angels were needed to nudge Neuhaus along that reality road.

Let me take you back to the Operating Room with me for a fresh vanity versus honesty metaphor. The other day I lay in a twilight zone—awake but sedated to the sawing and hammering as the space age materials replaced my old, necrotic right knee—and my mind began to shape an aphoristic essay, which I wrote down days later. Here is a clip from the essay:

> *The OR is a mystery to all but hospital staff. To the ordinary person it is that great chilled room one rolls into still conscious. It is a place of life and death decisions made at lightning speed.*
>
> *It tests one's faith to visualize health actually coming from the gothic slaughter on the floor of the room. That OR moment for me is what St. Francis meant. That in dying we live.*

A Little of That Goes a Long Way

Lynn: Surely we need not go to the OR or ER to really get it? Sounds pretty extreme. Besides not everyone can go there.

Darrel: Of course we may not literally need to go there. But the OR is more of a metaphor here. We may only need something that parallels an OR experience. Maybe like my friend, Judi, on a flight across the country. Soon after takeoff, the pilot announced that there were serious mechanical problems with the aircraft. He gave passengers about twenty minutes to prepare for the worst.

For Judi and the rest this was it—final prayers, mental goodbyes to family and friends, and the *certain reality of her own death approaching at warp speed.* However, a half hour later, they landed safely! But Judi emailed her friends that her life was changed forever. I would call that her triage moment.

Kierkegaard spoke of living life from its end, backward not forward. We get better appreciation for life looking back at it from the perspective of death than looking forward from birth.

Ballpark Concessions

Lynn: Yes, that rings true for me. A year ago in January I woke up in the ER and didn't know how I got there. At first the doctors thought it was a TIA or mini-stroke. Massive tests found it to be nothing that serious. Nevertheless, I guess this scare could be called a triage for me. Mortality grabbed center stage—and sharpened my perception of my fleeting life. It has actually left some lasting changes in my priorities—and even in my lifestyle.

Darrel, when we first became friends, I guess I thought I was going to help you walk through your last months and be there for you while your were dying. But somehow, it is I who feel most helped by our friendship. You definitely are nudging me out of the illusion of perceived permanence and I think you are helping position me to finish strong. So I really do hope I can reciprocate as you (and I) keep walking toward the inevitable.

Healthy Conversation

Darrel: *[Again waggling his eye-brows and flashing his patented grin]* Well my pilgrim friend, I definitely feel you walking with me—this spirited conversation has meant more to me than you can ever know.

But let's go back to our point: fear of death is a very real and enormously disorienting emotion. I certainly do not want to minimize it. However, most people I have talked with do not fear the fact of dying so much as they fear the how of dying. An article by Robin Marantz Henig gives at least one perspective on how we die.[6]

Many formulate their wish lists of how-I-want-to-die, which include such things as:

- dying quickly, but not too quickly so farewells can be made
- dying with a minimum of pain
- dying without losing control (physically or mentally—that is without pampers or straitjackets), and
- dying without becoming a burden (emotionally, financially, or physically) on family or friends.

Of course, these are also on my wish list, too. They seem fairly universal. However, the fear I speak of is not fear in the typical use of the word. Rather it is a deeper dread that some philosophers call true fear. It is dreading the loss of self—extinction of existence—and this relates again to the traps at death's door.

Challenging cultural assumptions—about busyness, consumerism, and youthfulness—require daunting levels of encouragement and thought. This is one major battleground for the inner life of our humanity. And in this war for our souls, both of us would do well to periodically seek another person's take on us to help us sniff around for whiffs of denial—someone who is honest enough to holler, "Watch out for that trap door!"

This is another back-drop against which we play out the S-aging drama.

Again, Darrel grins and his eyebrows dance—the curtain falls and the house-lights go up.

Suggestions for a Strong Finish

To begin moving deeper into the art of S-aging, write out a sentence or two in response to the following questions:

- What tricks or smoke and mirrors do you think you may have tried in order to stop your aging?

- Provided that busy life authentically helps you live until you die, how has it also kept you from looking at finishing strong?

Powerline

S-aging (growing old gracefully and intentionally) is not a luxury but a real human need to examine our lifestyle, our life goals, beginning at midpoint and periodically across the rest of our lifetime.

Helps

Put your finger in a bucket of water and then pull it out. How much impact did you have on the water?

- You may have had a small impact, but how long did it last?
- How long will you last?
- How long will your accomplishments last?
- Write a brief paragraph applying this lesson to your life (be positive and try to avoid being either cynical or appropriately modest.)

THREE MASTER PROMPTERS

. . . who keep us on script and
remind us of our lines

Chapter Seven

MEET THE MASTER PROMPTERS

"Age ain't nothin' but a number. But age is other things too. It is wisdom, if one has lived one's life properly. It is experience and knowledge. And it is getting to know all the ways the world turns, so that if you cannot turn the world the way you want, you can at least get out of the way so you won't get run over."

—MIRIAM MAKEBA [1]

KEY QUESTION: Who might be a life mentor to you?

Scene 7

As the curtain rises, Darrel and Lynn lean against the rail of the second floor veranda, at dawn of a new day. For a long while neither speaks as they quietly watch fresh light wash over the Texas Hill Country. Eventually Darrel pulls a sheet of paper from his notebook, studies it a moment, and turns to Lynn.

Darrel: I've been reading again from *The Jack London Reader*. Listen to his haunting voice from a short story called "To Build a Fire." The main character is looking back over an endless snow packed trail on the Yukon River during the Alaska gold rush. Here's what he says:

> He was a newcomer in the land, a chechaquo, and this was his first winter. The trouble with him was that he was without imagination. He was quick and alert in the things of life, but only in things, and not in the significances.
>
> Fifty degrees below zero meant eighty-odd degrees of frost. Such fact impressed him as being cold and uncomfortable, and that was all. It did not lead him to meditate upon his frailty as a creature of temperature, and upon man's frailty in general, able only to live within certain narrow limits of heat and cold; and from there on it did not lead him to the conjectural field of immortality and man's place in the universe . . . that there should be anything more to it than that [cold and uncomfortable] was a thought that never entered his head. [2]

Lynn: *[scratching his morning stubble]* Sounds like a portrait of too many American males: living in a world of *things or stuff* rather than in a world of *meanings*. But we need significant meanings—especially in the last periods of life. So Darrel, maybe for a healthy life S-ager, the gold rush of our early years will be followed by the meaning rush of our S-aging years.

Darrel: Yes, aging is mandatory. But both wisdom and significance remain optional. We can choose, however, to move beyond *things* to ponder and appreciate their deeper *meanings*—from things to transcendence—without which, in London's words, "imagination is dead."

Robert Fulghum wrote *Everything I Need to Know I Learned in Kindergarten*. It is a cute notion, but don't believe it. There are many very important deeper meanings to learn throughout all of life—especially in the later years. And we learn most of them from three Master Teachers—or I like to think of them as three Prompters whispering (some days even shouting) from the wings. The names of these Master Prompters are *Suffering, Relationships,* and *Dying.*

Actually, it was Richard P. Johnson, a geriatric psychologist who gave these words to my own experience. He said that "in healthy aging there are *only three* great or master teachers—*suffering, relationships*, and *death*."[3]

For me that was a WOW statement! Of course, I thought, through these three I have come to harvest life's most profound lessons. *Suffering, relationships, and dying* send in our lines and keep us on script as we play out the S-aging drama on the stage of life.

My problem is not listening well. When I muff my lines (or resist the lines I've been handed!), I'm tempted to block out the prompters—and ad lib. It is my nature to shut off the panic; to emotionally isolate myself. The upside of this: it can keep me steady under fire. The downside: it sometimes hinders me from experiencing the full, rich measure of my humanity.

I believe we learn and grow to the extent that we hear the prompters. To the extent we ignore them, we stagnate or shrivel.

I have since personalized this concept and expanded it—perhaps in different directions than Richard Johnson himself intended.

- To this person whose own problems and angst had been the wellspring of most of my new self-understandings—*suffering* is a prompter.
- To this person who experiences both the love and the challenges of sustaining a family circle, and/or life-long friendships—*relationships* is a prompter.
- As a dying person communicating with other dying persons—*death* is a prompter.

Coming Closer to Home

Darrel: But no one said these Master Prompters were easy. They are often hard, sometimes cruel, teachers. Consequently, some of us get stuck in the pain and miss the growth and depth it could bring. My brother got stuck in the quicksand of despair and bitterness. He had been a wonderful brother. Near genius. Endlessly creative. Adventuresome. His imagination seeded mine. He was three years older, so his big brother escapades and Huckleberry Finn-like flights of boyhood fantasy filled my childhood with color.

Then as adults we grew apart. He led an exotic life in medicine and the military, but then in the last decades withdrew from the family, becoming a recluse. He viewed the world as dark and sinister. We became estranged over what seemed trivial to me.

When my brother became terminally ill, I traveled to another state to visit him. Over several days, I reviewed memories and thanksgiving, primarily for myself I think, but for him too. Inexplicably he abruptly broke off the conversation. And with some heat, he said, "It would be best if you go home now."

Somewhere on the journey my brother lost his way—and wandered into the dark valley called "dying badly." I feel a sad burden to this day. And all the more determined to die well. In a strange way I hear my brother's dying voice prompting from the wings.

When Robert Fulghum said, "Everything I needed to know I learned in kindergarten," it seemed he forgot the possibility of a second ironic childhood:

S-aging. Ah no, Mr. Fulghum, the best lessons of life are to be learned not in kindergarten, but in the experiences of aging. The Master Prompters take up long after kindergarten leaves off. The richest scenes to be played out on the stage of life can be those final S-aging scenes.

Lynn: *[With pencil, writing on a pad the preamble for this section of the book]* Having met the Prompters, we will try to walk beside them one by one. And we will do our best to hear the urgency in their voices.

With that, the curtain falls on this scene.

Sage Suggestions for a Strong Finish

Tips for Finishing Strong

Three voices from offstage speak lines to us:

- Suffering holds the potential of growth through pain.
- Relationships hold the potential for growth through our connectedness to others.

- Dying (the process and not the moment) holds the potential to frame the profound truth of our whole life.

Powerline

Without the prompters of life we will often stand agape on stage wondering when the audience will begin to hiss.

A Semi-serious Review (multiple answer):

1. The authors spent most of their careers—
    a. in jail
    b. writing this book
    c. in pulpits
2. Age-ism is:
    a. A disease of historians
    b. The addictive pursuit of antiques
    c. Bias against older persons
3. Two of the Three Prompters are:
    a. Arthritis
    b. Suffering
    c. Relationships
    Name the Third Prompter_______________

And a Preview

The rest of the book will offer the following topics and challenges:

1. A survey of the *Three Master Prompters* and the *Three Major Issues* of Life—mortality, identity, and legacy,
2. A serious challenge to the reader to begin acting fully alive to their future, and an ending stuffed with stories of successful persons and vitalizing tips for S-aging.

Proceed.

Chapter Eight

FIRST MASTER PROMPTER: SUFFERING

Lines whispered by the first prompter: "The man who has not suffered, what does he know anyway?"

—Rabbi Abraham Heschel

KEY QUESTION: How has your latest bout with illness, grief, or catastrophe changed you?

Scene 8

Lynn and his wife, Carolyn, have come to visit Darrel and his wife, Barbara, in Georgetown, Texas, where the Gibertsons now live.

Lynn: Are you ready to pick up with that first Prompter?

Darrel: *Suffering.* My definition of suffering includes *all the ordinary pains of life* (although a lot of these little pains are merely inconveniences) *as well as the catastrophic physical or emotional slams.* In the hardscrabble landscape of the s-aging process the suffering lessons are rarely learned quickly. You can't cook them in the microwave. How about sixty or seventy years of hard baking?

Darrel looks at the back of his left hand and rubs it with his right.

Recently my daughter, Kari, called to say, "Dad, you really had a hard job." Earlier that day a Texas State Trooper and a police chaplain had interrupted her music judging contest. And Kari stood by listening as the police chaplain broke the terrible news to one of the judges that her husband had just been killed in an auto accident. From point blank range, Kari witnessed the enormous impact of suffering. She said it dawned on her that I, as a pastor, had done this numerous times. Kari was beginning to taste the bitter soul-shaping force of suffering.

Lynn: No question that *Suffering* whispers valuable lines, though I suspect that some people might choke on that idea—unless they have been through *great suffering.* Darrel, from where I sit, you are in considerable *suffering.* What is this Master Prompter whispering to you?

Darrel: I cannot deny there are times when I don't want to hear this raspy whisper from the wings. Of course, the steepest learning curve that suffering has thrown me personally so far was the diagnosis of a fatal illness. Yet I know that more and worse suffering lies not too far ahead. But maybe repeatedly overhearing this prompter speak to others across the years (as have you) has partly prepared me to hear Suffering speak personally to me. For example, once a district attorney called me at 2 A.M. asking if a certainly family were members of our church. Their only son had just died in the worst auto accident in North Dakota history—eight teenagers killed in carnage on Interstate 94. So at 4 A.M. in the morning I felt my way thirty miles out into a dark prairie landscape to a farm house. The porch light was on when I drove up the lane. The father came out to the car and said he knew why I was there. He had been listening to a police radio band. I found myself in the middle of this family's white hot pain as suffering screamed from the wings. I think their suffering, and many similar experiences, helped prepare me for this suffering of my own.

Of course, *some* suffering can be prevented. Dumb choices can bring miserable results. But there are large sufferings that cannot be avoided, no matter how smart our choices. Sometimes bad things *do* happen to good people!

What Suffering Can Teach Us

Whatever the cause or kind of suffering, this Master Prompter whispers big lessons—if we have ears to listen! An ancient Bible character by the name of Job was listening!

Lynn: Along with Job, in the Bible, I would nominate Shakespeare's Hamlet as one of literature's great sufferers—who suffers and puzzles.

Whether it is nobler in the mind to suffer the slings and arrows of outrageous fortunes—or to take arms against a sea of troubles and by opposing, end them.[1]

When we are confronted with these outrageous fortunes, rather than copping out, we can step up. But not everyone steps up. Darrel, I wonder, how we really listen to hear what *Suffering* is trying to tell us? Or to become what *Suffering* is trying to grow us into?

Darrel: Two words: *vulnerable . . . undaunted.* About an identical event, the Northern Germans will say, "It is serious but not fatal," but the Southern Germans will opine, "It is fatal but not serious." I prefer the Southern philosophy. It has true grit!

But maybe more importantly, *Suffering can be Redemptive.*

A big word, I know, and a religious one to boot. I simply mean: *suffering is not pointless*. Good can be wrung from evil's grasp. The baddest lemon can make the bestest batch of lemonade!

Words of Redemption

Darrel: For example, in the Old Testament: Joseph's heartless brothers sold him into slavery. But years later, Joseph had become virtually a prince in Egypt, and ironically his starving brothers' only hope for food. When reunited with his estranged brothers Joseph observed, "You intended to harm me, but God intended it for good to accomplish what is now being done, the saving of many lives."[2]

Long term, Joseph's suffering brought huge redemptive value—for both him and his brothers. I also see redemptive suffering at the very heart of the Christian story: Judas betrays Jesus to death on a cross. But God turns the cross into forgiveness and hope.

Lynn: *[gesturing out to the people walking in Boerne Market]* What about these people? How can we once again bring this closer to home, Darrel? What specific redemptive values have come to you personally out of your current greatest suffering? You once mused over St. Paul's words, "after I have preached to others, I myself might become a castaway."[3]

When you were first diagnosed, and we had some of our first conversations about your state of mind, I wrote in my journal some of what you said:

Darrel told me, "It is possible to die in a terrible absence of God. I have waffled and wobbled—and wondered: Am I quitting on life before I can afford to quit—am I losing my nerve?

I have some good days, very good. But then I have some bad days. Sometimes I fear loss of powers even fear incontinence. Some nights are filled with incriminating dreams. Faults, failings, sins, painfully begin to surface.

I don't want to lose my nerve. Mother lost her nerve after Dad died."

When I asked you what you meant by losing your nerve you answered:

"If I lost nerve I may enter Sheol, the shade. (not hell or brimstone, but a place of half-life, here and now.) I might slide into a vacuum—die before I'm dead. Get where I do not enjoy books or ideas. Rather than feeling excited about an idea, sort of look at it as road kill.

Loss of nerve might leave me with no real laughter or real sense of humor. Or where I am not interested in my granddaughter Sophia's latest adventures. Or feigning interest in people's stories.

I am not talking about clinical depression here, but a real existential state; what Luther called the great terrible sin of despair. For the dying, I see a horse race between despair and faith."

Darrel, that was nearly five years ago. What has *Suffering* taught you since then?

Moving Into the Future

Darrel: I am at quite a different place now, for which I am deeply grateful. Now, these years later, I have evidence that I likely won't sink into the arms of the evil twins (despair and withdrawal). Rather if I am afraid, it is the fear of missing *the excitement of new things:* the adventure of positive, hopeful living. As Paul the Apostle said, "leaving the past behind, I press on."[4] I don't want to miss that pressing on!

You know, Lynn, I am a work in progress. I think I am actually finishing much stronger than what I feared two years ago. That onerous voice has helped prompt me to this place.

Lynn: Congratulations! [*applauding*] You wrote a very cogent essay about hearing your diagnosis and its impact in the years since. Originally you entitled it "Looking Down into My Own Grave." But you explained that the point is the looking, not the grave. I am guessing it was your Hamlet-wannabe soliloquy on Finishing Strong & Dying Well.

[Lynn reads Darrel's essay aloud]

I was not in the room when the doctor announced my fatal illness and my impending demise. I was in the O.R. recovery. My family was told "Darrel is a very sick man—the liver stones blocking the main bile ducts need to be removed. But the overall condition is not reversible. He may have two years or less to live."

A couple days later my wife told me the bad news. There was an initial, mind-numbed silence. As a pastor for well over thirty years I had delivered such news to others countless times. Yet, no one is a veteran at receiving this. Trust me.

But curiously, after the initial shock the thought came to me: This is how I will die. When I tell people this I can see pity in their eyes and can almost see them thinking: He doesn't have a clue! *Truthfully I too wondered if I had missed something.*

Lynn: How have your feelings and thoughts changed since then?

The Years Since

Darrel: Today? This much I can tell you for sure: I did not keep staring down into my own grave. With time, I just put one foot in front of the other and continued the walk I call life. And my perspective has kept changing ever since. Actually, what began with some shock and maybe a bit of fear and morbidity has now just become a part of life, of who I am.

Barbara's journey has been different, however. More than five years later Barbara confessed that she has only recently fully faced my death. I conclude two things from that: first (and you have been saying this), one cannot fully face another person's death even the death of a spouse. And second, Barbara made a judgment call not to borrow trouble from tomorrow by worrying. She would wait to see how it all played out. I cannot disagree with her call.

Now to myself: I am an evolving identity; a soul deepening with age. I will not accept credit for some heroic courage not due me. But I can tell you that I have changed. I am a happy camper, at peace with myself—and grateful for every day. I feel free! This has not come through just one single epiphany. Nor has it been a steady upward slope.

After I retired in 2000, we moved to an active retirement community, Sun City in Central Texas—which has proven to be a happy choice. About two years later was when I received a call inviting me to teach a course for Senior University (classes taught and supported by Sun City and greater Georgetown residents). I promised to call back the next morning. Oddly, on the patio the next morning, it occurred to me that since I am *dying*, I guess *that* could be a course I could teach (likely an idea incubating three years before it hatched.)

A Qualified Professor

Darrel: So, besides chronicling my own journey, I began a serious study of books about dying. What an expanding landscape with a receding horizon. (Amazon.com listed 127,448 books on a growing list!) Writing the presentations was enormously rewarding. I needed to do this for myself—even if no one else might be interested. I felt effervescent with newfound enthusiasm and, as you will recall, named my weird course "Finishing Strong & Dying Well."

The weekend before launch I called the Senior University office, silently praying that no one had signed up. I seldom blink at anything anymore—but the next words stunned me: "Mr. Gilbertson, your class drew a lot of interest and 33 registered!"

The bright and nimble minds of the students continued to amaze me: their compelling stories and the interest in my material. Since then I have taught several variations on that course, including one section Barbara and I co-taught, "For Women Only."

These courses gave focus to my grieving. They also give ongoing personal transformation and satisfaction to my life through the friendships that resulted, the couple-hood enrichment, and now this book that will grow out of it. All add up to a rich brew out of the millings of what you call my great suffering.

But still, I must definitely add, suffering has been ever so redemptive for me. But that certainly doesn't mean that I look forward to the rest of it!

Cautious Probing

Lynn: Darrel, forgive my incredulity, but have you ever caught yourself masking dread with positive platitudes?

Darrel: *[blinking then grinning]* You never let up, do you?

Hmm. Maybe so. At least in small blips. Bunyan haunts me here. Near the very gate of heaven in *Pilgrim's Progress* Bunyan has tricks and trapdoors that lead straight to hell. *My rocky road ahead looms difficult.* Life is never a done deal. I still fear having fears. So somehow I never fully escape the specter of a terrible regression into self-pity, isolation, withdrawal, and despair.

Strange, the eighth anniversary of my death sentence just passed. Sometimes I have felt twinges of guilt. Guilt for still being alive. But I find comfort in Stephen Hawking, the theoretical cosmologist who has lived with ALS (Lou Gehrig's disease) for over forty years! And he still lectures around the world with an artificial electronic voice.

It is a fight, but I think I am winning. So far, I daily find a way to dump these destructive feelings before I become a victim of them.

I chalk this up to God's grace. Faith is my traction on these slippery slopes. It overcomes my existential angst. My life counts for something because the banner over me is God's Love and love never fails nor ends. So be it.

Lynn: *[after a long pause]* I am sure you know that this exchange has been a bit uncomfortable for me. I would guess for you even more so. But thanks for providing this invaluable tutorial for me and, I hope, also for the folks sitting out in those theater seats. Suffering surely is a Master Prompter—if—if we really listen to her.

Sage Suggestions for a Strong Finish

How can one break through to a sense of peace about suffering? For starters, digest these axioms:

- Whether self-inflicted or accidental, suffering comes to all, even the most charmed.
- Suffering may soften at the edges by time, reflection, and a change of direction, plus it can be and often is transcended.
- Suffering underscores our finiteness and maximizes our vulnerabilities or limitations. But—the good news is this: suffering can be powerfully redemptive and also has the potential to exponentially expand our faith and character.
- But we must not ignore that fact that suffering in all its shapes and forms is intensely personal and unnerving.

POWERLINE

We do a terrible disservice to our children when we shelter them from the hard edges of life. Rather than shielding or rescuing them we might stand close by ready to encourage and cheer them through their valley of the shadow.

HELPS

A Tool for Self-Understanding and Suffering (Fill in the blank with the first thought that comes to mind)

1. I feel the low point in my whole life was the time when_______________
____

2. During this time I remember how someone encouraged me when I most needed it. They said ______________________________

____

3. One day I saw someone hurting and asked them if they wanted to share anything and they said to me____________________________

____

4. What I have learned from the Master Prompter called suffering is_____

____

Chapter Nine

SECOND MASTER PROMPTER: RELATIONSHIPS

Lines *spoken* by the second prompter

"When two people agree on everything, one of them is unnecessary."

—Carolyn Anderson

"I love humanity. It's the people I can't stand!"

—Charlie Brown

KEY QUESTION: When was the time you felt most hurt or betrayed in a relationship?

Scene 9

After an early lunch at a cafeteria in Georgetown, Texas, Lynn and Darrel pick up the conversation where they had left it earlier in the morning.

Lynn: I thought it more than a little curious that you put *relationships* in the same category as *suffering* among the master prompters.

Darrel: Yes, I seated relationships beside suffering. And they do seem like an odd couple, Lynn, but really they are not. If *suffering* teaches us by the sheer pain of our human limitations, then *relationships* teach by their rich but bewildering complexity.

I define that Second Prompter, *Relationships*, as the art of staying in healthy connection with others. Ah, but relationships bedevil us. They are nuanced with so many layers. Mysterious. They are never straight-line. Usually squiggly, in fact.

Some may find suffering and dying the most difficult and perverse prompters. But personally I find relationships to be the toughest teacher of all. Relationship building is a lifetime of work. What's your take, Lynn?

Lynn: I have not personally experienced much real suffering (though, like you, I have often observed it up close in others.) But it seems to me that relationships must be at least as challenging as suffering. Yet, in spite of their difficulty, I think a healthy relationship is worth every bit of the time and energy it takes. Relationships bring such joy and they teach wisdom as well.

Darrel: *[Pausing to brush a leaf off the table]* Lone, isolated people miss out on a lot. Truth is, however, r*elationships*—authentic relationships, that is—are definitely not easy. If relationships were simple the whole wide world would break out in pandemic harmony. But in reality, most of us muddle around through a daily grind of conflicted connections with the other.

Challenges of Otherness

Lynn: *[nodding agreement]* Yes! Bewildering. Challenging too—partly because each relationship is unique.

I think the most challenging relationship of all may be marriage: where even the slightest flicker of an eyelash can profoundly impact the other person. To make it work demands more learning and giving than pretty much any other relationship. Yet it is so bewildering that, even in a lifetime of learning we never seem to master it! Probably no other relationship has near the potential for misery—or for joy.

Darrel: I sometimes wonder if I have some kind of amnesia. For example: Once in college I forgot my future wife's birthday.

[Again, the waggling eyebrows and grin]

Once was enough.

This past year I made a huge effort to celebrate our forty-third wedding anniversary and our half-century as Valentine's Day sweethearts. We made reservations at a fine restaurant, a day of antiquing, then a B&B in the countryside. A wonderful Valentines Day, but still I would give myself only a B minus on this year's efforts. Marriage continues to humble me.

Lynn: Me too. What's more, each marriage is unique. No two marriages work exactly alike. My wife Carolyn takes a dim view of self-help books with titles like *Five Keys to a Happier Marriage* and *Ten Steps to Restoring Romance*. She says that persons are too unique and relationships too complex for simple one-size-fits-all rules.

Our fingerprints give us a clue that God breaks every mold He uses. And this God-designed one-of-a-kind-ness runs far beyond our fingertips throughout our emotional histories and into our one-of-a-kind original souls. Put two unique and complex souls together—and you definitely have a challenging one-of-a-kind relationship. Sure, some broad commonalities run across most human relationships. But each specific marriage relationship is far too unique and bewildering for plug and play formulas. In fact, Carolyn's favorite marriage book is *The Mystery of Marriage* by Mike Mason. Mason says each marriage is its own work of art, made up of the mysteries of its own special journey.

Of course the marriage relationship may be the most challenging and instructive of all. But then aren't all relationships challenging master prompters?

Darrel: Yes. I see all relationships as crucibles for character training—but only if we pay attention to them, work at them, and feed them healthy foods. They feed on honesty and caring. On give and take. On openness and fairness. Investing in relationships keeps us on a relentless learning and growing curve.

High Risk Venture

Darrel: Yes, genuine relationships, like all of life's best ecstasies, are also high maintenance ventures. That means they are also high risk ventures. They are a big investment in time and emotion—and you can lose it all. But as Barbara, a keen observer of the human situation, says, "Life favors the risk-takers."

Lynn: I would definitely vote with Barbara on that one. If safety and security become too highly valued, relationships can become numbingly pedestrian—and life very shallow besides. As Teddy Roosevelt said, "Far better it is to dare mighty things, to win glorious triumphs even though checkered by failure, than to rank with those poor spirits who neither enjoy nor suffer much because they live in the gray twilight that knows neither victory nor defeat."[1]

Darrel: Consider too the wide array of skills that healthy relationships call into play, not the least of which is *peacemaking*. Remember the four stages?

During both *Ages or Scenes Three and Four,* the making and sharing of peace—especially interpersonal peace (i.e. relationship management)—is a hallmark of healthy S-aging. The sages across the ages have prayed to own this skill. Most notable was St. Francis of Assisi. Remember his lines:

Lord, make us instruments of your peace.
Where there is hatred, let us sow love;
where there is injury, pardon;
where there is discord, union;
where there is doubt, faith;
where there is despair, hope;
where there is darkness, light
where there is sadness, joy.
Grant that we may seek, not so much
to be consoled as to console;
to be understood as to understand;
to be loved as to love.[2]

Confronting vs. Bullying

Darrel: But of course, the plan of St. Francis runs counter to our culture and to my own temperament as well. Our hubris rewards intimidation tactics and urges us to bully. I confess at my weakest moments I too easily give in to our culture of intimidation. It is my base nature. Doctors warn me that my autoimmune system is in poor shape medically, but it is spiritually that I need a boost of immunity against the bully temptation. In fact, just recently a dear friend told me politely to back off because I was pushing my point so relentlessly.

One big part of my finishing strong is learning to dial back my over-assertiveness.

Lynn: Bingo, another way we are alike. But healthy relationships still must, as David Augsburger says, "care enough to confront."[3] Stephen Covey urges, "Seek first to *understand*. Then to be *understood. But seek both!*"[4] Otherwise, while somebody wins, somebody also loses. Over the long haul, merely passively choosing always to lose erodes healthy relationships just as surely as bullying does. However, there is a vast difference between bullying and healthy confronting. Confronting expresses differences honestly, but in respectful ways—seeking both understanding and to be understood—all the while working toward win/win. Bullying, as you say, seeks only to win. A real relationship smasher. Is it too much to hope, Darrel, that S-aging might actually grow the bully instinct out of both of us?

Darrel: Well, I do have firsthand experience at the wrong kind of confrontation. Recently I lost my peacemaking balance and shouted at a picketer on the property of our current housing development. Then I spiraled down into stubborn dismissal of the other person. I was not proud of myself.

However, I am learning. At least in one better moment, I sensed that a tie vote would lead only to more dysfunctional behavior in a small rural church where I was an interim pastor. So I offered a biblical method for resolving the deadlock: Let's draw straws. They accepted, parish civil war was avoided, and both sides were at least politely happy with the outcome. Blessed are the peacemakers.[5]

Win-Win and Collaboration

Lynn: Wonderful, but oh so difficult: to reach win-win. However, Stephen Covey says we must go beyond respectful *confronting,* though, to genuine *col-*

laborating. Where we synergize our strengths, so that both of us can win even bigger than either of us could win alone.[6]

Darrel: I like that word *collaborate.* Collaboration is not mere group-think. It is group doing some thinking—creating by shared perspective. And a byproduct beyond win/win is a circle of valued relationships—maybe even involving some shared accomplishments!

Lynn: Speaking of groups, participating in an ongoing group—a little community—keeps us growing. Men especially, whether we acknowledge it or not, need a circle of close friends who can explore new horizons together and grow as iron sharpens iron. Plus we need close loyal friends with whom we can entrust confidences.

Help is All Around Us

Darrel: I really agree. My "Men Only" class taught me the value of the small group process. When the formal classes ended, most of the men actually continued their group experiences in ongoing clusters of four to five persons. I did not coach them in this. It just came about.

[Darrel sits up and waves his hands; discussing this kind of collaboration nearly lifts him off his chair as he explains that such group formation has become a key strategy in coaching men toward S-aging.]

Anyone can do this. He or she can find another person or two and start his or her own group—then add others as you go. I urge them to pick a topic at first. Set rules for engagement and commit to meet regularly with purpose. (For some "Rules for Collaborative Engagement" in these groups, see the exercise at end of this chapter.)

Lynn: Great strategy! I have found that an excellent way to get started is for each person to tell his or her own story. My leadership coaching groups are ten to fourteen persons, who meet monthly for a year. We always begin the year telling our stories (no matter how many group sessions it takes to hear every person's story.) And anyone can do this. It doesn't take looks, brains, talent, or money—yet the results are almost magical. Deeper trust. Strong bonding. Fresh openness. Plus rich and lasting learning.[7]

Darrel: I have found that the shared wisdom of others often nudged me past dead spots in my career development. And now during retirement, in my quest to finish strong, I continue to tap the riches of older minds and fellow S-agers.

In the high trust of long-term relationships, we find the noblest and best of ourselves. And I have even found that genuine, unconditional love is not as rare as some male cultural stereotypes suggest.

The Blessings of Otherness

Darrel: Yet as you said earlier, Lynn, in spite of the cost, healthy relationships are worth it. In spite of some agony, there is also much ecstasy. Hanging on your wall I saw that copy of a document purportedly found in old Saint Paul's church, Baltimore, dated 1629:

> As far as possible without surrender be on good terms with all persons . . . With all its sham, drudgery and broken dreams, this is still a beautiful world.
>
> But the beauty is usually more obvious to those who travel in the company of others.[8]

Lynn: So true. So very true.

The stage light dims and the curtains close.

Sage Suggestions for a Strong Finish

List three things that your own *relationships* have been trying to teach you.

1. ______________________________
2. ______________________________
3. ______________________________

Helps

So you want to begin a small collaborative group:

1. Some group formats useful to help Finish Strong & Die Well?
    - *a. Discovery Groups* that explore in order to expand understanding of an issue and appreciation of each person's viewpoints. (Evaluate books, movies, articles, lectures together.)
    - *b. Life Enrichment Groups* to deepen relationships. Develop transparency in order to overcome isolation and loneliness.
    - *c. Journey Editing Groups* that monitor each other's written history or biographical material for stage clarification and path re-direction.
2. Some questions to answer as you shape your collaborative group
    - a. *How will we handle confidentiality?* With spouses or friends alike, the answer to what did you talk about is general—Today we talked about a movie or book and its message. Period.
    - b. *What is the optimal size?* Five to seven seems to work best. This leaves some room for some shrinkage or absenteeism.
    - c. *What format shall we use for each session?* Open with hospitality concerns and continue with connecting (relational) questions and bonding strategies. At a coffee house, home setting, retreat center.
    - d. *How often should we meet?* Not less than once a month. Twice a month is better. But break for vacations and holidays.
    - e. *How shall we handle disagreements?* Make the group safe for disagreements. Always agree to let someone disagree with another member of the group without being disagreeable.
    - f. *Do I have to sign a covenant of something?* Formal statements seem stuffy. But, some well thought out Rules of Engagement can be helpful.

Chapter Ten

THIRD MASTER PROMPTER: DYING

A *shout* from the third prompter

Someone who is always thinking about happiness is a fool;
a wise person thinks about death.

ECCLESIASTES 7:4 (TEV)

KEY QUESTION: How can our end be our beginning?

Scene 10

At 6 A.M., Lynn finds early riser, Darrel, on the front porch with his usual steaming cup of Scandinavian nectar in one hand and the newspaper in the other. Then right there, in the freshness of the morning air, Darrel begins cheerily to talk about dying. Bam! Just like that! The Third Prompter is Dying.

Still feeling awkward approaching death so abruptly, so head-on with a man who knew he was dying, Lynn fumbles for an appropriate response. He stiffly reads words from an old book:

Lynn: "How large a part death plays in all of life's considerations! And yet how very little we know about it! History establishes death to be a universal fact. Biology offers a scientific explanation: simple transition of elements. Philosophy describes death as a state of non-being. Poetry hovers over the casket on trembling wings of eloquence only to quickly flee in shivering terror. All contributions to the theme are marked by the same essential vagueness."[1]

[Both men sit quietly. Darrel nods after hearing words so formal—and dark.]

Darrel: This much we do know: dying is *inevitable.* The human death rate stays at one hundred percent. We are both dying you know.

But I believe that when we come to grips with our own dying and face it head-on, the prospect of impending death can actually enrich us. But let me hone definitions a bit. Death can be distinguished from dying itself. *Death* is a generic or abstract idea. *Dying* is an intensely personal experience. Most people I meet do not fear *death* so much as they do *dying*. We all know that dying looks like a bummer, on the surface of it.

Lynn: *[Still feeling awkward and relapsing into stiff reading]* "The only feeling death has to offer is a broken heart. The only flowers death offers are wilting petals on a forgotten grave. The only sound : a muffled sob—and the crunch of footsteps slowly retreating from the cemetery."[2]

And dying seems *so final*. "Grass soon grows over us, the winds of time blow across the place, till all who once remembered us are themselves gone and forgotten."[3]

Darrel: Eight years have passed since the doctors said the statistical probability of my death was two years. I was struck a blow then, but somehow I did not blink. Maybe it would have been better if I had. But at the time I believed that, since my own dying is inevitable, why should I consider it a tragedy? I still believe that.

But I guess the real shocker is timing: death comes "like a thief in the night," as the Bible says. Yet, I feel fortunate because I spotted my thief ahead of time. I have had some time to ponder life's finish, which gives me a better shot at finishing strong. As the ancient poet said, "So teach us to number our days aright, that we may gain a heart of wisdom."[4]

That wisdom includes shifting one way to deal with dying. As Betty Freidan puts it in her book, *Fountain of Age*, "the developmental tasks of late life involve a clear shift from the values of youth."[5]

Making a Shift

Lynn: *[finally putting his book down]* Darrel, describe how this clear shift from the values of youth changed your S-aging journey? What followed the initial shock of your diagnosis?

Darrel: Well, first off, Barb and our whole family researched Primary Sclerosing Cholangitis, the condition with which I was diagnosed. PSC is a companion disease to ulcerative colitis. It is idiopathic, having no clear cause. And at the time I was diagnosed, possibly two—but not more than five years—was thought to be the life expectancy. Walter Peyton of the Chicago Bears had an almost identical condition. He went on the *Oprah* show appealing for a liver transplant, but died in his forties.

In her book, *Middlemarch,* George Elliot has Dorothea Causaubon pleading with her husband's doctor to help Mr. Causaubon shift from his obsessive activity to a sedentary lifestyle to persevere his health: "Oh, you are a wise man, are you not? You know all about life and death. Advise me. Think what I can do. He has been laboring all his life and looking forward. He minds about nothing else. And I mind about nothing else—"[6] My wife Barb could well have spoken these exact words to my doctors in those first forced retirement months.

I had a death sentence! Yet in the seven years since, inexplicably, I cannot remember a five-minute feel-sorry-for-me party or a day of depression. Is that weird? Or is there some other explanation?" (By the way, more recent research says PSC life expectancy is now six to twelve years.)

[Darrel pauses for a long time] My shift was nudged along during my death diagnosis. I had two superb doctors—both happened to be Jewish (like Jesus!). They were both professional to the hilt—yet they were treating me like a revered Rabbi Emeritus. Whenever I profusely thanked them for their attentive care, they would point toward the sky and say, "God heals; I am just His instrument." Their self-effacing words were a tonic! Just what I needed to hear. The beginning of my *true healing*. Not Pollyanna babblings of false hopes. But words of genuine soul healing.

As I left the hospital a few days later, now aware of my prognosis, I almost skipped to the car—in the best of spirits. I had already moved beyond the limp so-this-is-the-way-I-will-die kind of tone, shifting toward a granite-hard with-God's-help-I-can-do-this. I *can* finish strong & die well.

Lynn: But I have to ask again, Just how do you now account for that? Not everyone receives such bad news so honestly, so analytically, and—forgive me—so triumphantly.

Thunderstruck

Darrel: I think you have good reason to keep re-cycling that question. Obviously I have answered it a bit differently at various stages of my journey. So I need to keep re-visiting that question. Actually, I'm not so sure myself. It is extremely humbling to me—and a source of wonder, even of awe. On a surface level it may have sprung from my lifelong habit of a deal-with-it-mentality? Or—more honestly—maybe at times it was a tweaked perspective of Ernest Becker's *The Denial of Death.* Or (best case scenario) maybe it was a harvest-of-faith? The doctors pointed me back in the right direction you know—looking up. Maybe that steeled me for hearing the crunch on gravel of steps walking away from my cemetery plot. This much I can tell you for sure: till this day, by God's grace I honestly haven't played the game of sentimentalism or idealized my legacy.

Embracing Ambiguity

Lynn: *[After a long silence]* Of course I want to believe that people of faith deal with dying better than folks without God in the equation. However this isn't always the case. I have seen radically different reactions to the fatal diagnosis among people of faith. For example, two friends of mine, both visible and respected Christian leaders, died with cancer within a few months of each other. One had been a gregarious and positive thinking person for a lifetime, yet spent his dying months in panic and morbid depression. The other, who had lived life with a low-key and almost somber demeanor, spent his dying months with grace and encouragement to others. I don't know how to explain this.

Darrel: Well that truly *is* a troubling question. I ponder it often, though not in a desperate sort of way. For one thing, it may be simply that people are wired up differently, and each does travel his or her own unique emotional trail. And of course I do wonder how meaningful my experience would be to another dying person. Yet at the same time, I believe that—at least for me—faith makes the difference in the equation.

Something Bigger

Lynn: Some intellectual heavyweights seem to agree. For example, you mentioned that Freud's protégé, Otto Rank, a hardnosed man of science, raised the eyebrows of his colleagues when he declared that "Man is a *theological* creature, not just a *biological* one."[7] I hear Rank saying that human beings are *spiritual* beings, not just *physical* creatures.

Darrel: Yes, Rank confirms my conviction that any life experience which excludes the transcendent dimension is incomplete. I firmly believe that "God is MY refuge and strength, a very present help in trouble."[8] I know I can never be cured physically, but that is totally okay. Still, I am whole. I am healed.

We both know skeptical friends who began to have some theological thoughts when they began to face death. God may have been in their equation more than they had previously been aware. Few people feel satisfied facing death believing that this short and often disappointing physical existence is all there is to a human being. That idea seems obscene.

Lynn: *[grinning]* I am feeling a literary spell coming on again. Robert J. Ingersoll comes to mind here. Ingersoll was a famous nineteenth-century agnostic and critic of Christian faith, yet in a eulogy at his much loved brother's funeral Ingersoll couldn't help but glance upwards:

> Life is but a narrow vale between the cold and barren peaks of two eternities. We strive in vain to see beyond the heights. We cry aloud, but the only answer is the echo of our wailing cry, for from the voice-less lips of the un-replying dead there comes no sound. *But watching, hope can see a star, and faith can hear the rustle of a wing.*[9]

Darrel, obviously faith plays a dominant role in your S-aging drama. Mine too.

From Over Near the Exit

Lynn: From over here nearer the exit, the wisdom literature of the Old Testament especially reminds me that God is the beginning of all wisdom. This is the *mantra* of Ecclesiastes. Actually for years, I saw the Philosopher Sage of Ecclesiastes as a hardcore cynic—who likely died a bitter man. However, gradually, I grew to appreciate the rigor of his honesty—and the need for my own—and to be content with the modesty of his conclusion and the winsome ambiguity of his hope. Like him, I hold onto faith at the center—without Pollyanna scripted answers or pie-in-the-sky promises. I think the faith that serves us best is modest in its conclusions, and less than fanciful in the hope it offers—but solid and undaunted at its core.

Darrel: *[looking across the hills, squinting, then turning back to Lynn]* Yes, from over nearer the exit, I guess I am suggesting that for me, relational faith (the *Presence)* actually seems indispensable, if I am to finish strong & die well. At least for me.

But we certainly don't want to ignore the experience of some who appear to die quite well without faith.

The curtain falls and the houselights rise.

Sage Suggestions For A Strong Finish

Comment on the following statements.

- "*You cannot over-estimate the un-importance of almost everything.*" [10]
- *Death will always remain an enemy,* but not an unexpected stranger.
- It is not just facing the *prospect* of *death*, however, but *appropriating the inevitability of death* that is indeed the beginning of wisdom.

Powerline

We are all in hospice long before we arrive at that time.

Get used to it.

Helps

The following is a sentence completion recommended by hospice workers. But these questions are useful at any point in life!

In your preparation to finish strong & die well, how would you complete the following sentences?[11]

1. I thank . . .
2. I love . . .
3. I thank . . .
4. I ask you to forgive (or I regret) . . .
5. I forgive . . .
6. I bless (or I say goodbye to) . . .

PLOT

S-Aging is the primary plot.
However, three intriguing sub-plots are woven around it, without which there is no meaningful S-aging drama.

The sub-plots:

Mortality

Identity

Legacy

Chapter Eleven

SUB-PLOT 1—MORTALITY

When I was a kid my mother said: "There are certain things, Joseph, you don't talk about in polite company. You don't talk about politics, don't talk about religion, you don't talk about sex." She never said death, but I would add that . . . I think it is a topic that needs to be discussed so that we can get our fears and our anxieties out in front of us, take a look at them, and then begin to deal with them.

—Studs Terkel[1]

KEY QUESTION: So why must I face death?

Scene 11

Lynn and Darrel are driving through Texas Hill Country, savoring the rugged scenery—talking again about life and death. This scene opens as they sit in a roadside restaurant, vigorously discussing their different aging perspectives.

Of Patina and Old Rocks

Darrel: Lynn, although you are two years older than I am, I wonder if you lack for *S-aging patina*. Let me explain. Before my first trip to Italy, a friend told me to look for the Florentine patina—a certain aging quality of the stone structures in Florence. When I first looked across the Arno River from the old center city, I immediately saw it—patina—a subtle, but certain color cast peculiar to those ancient Mediterranean cities that adds a rustic, burnished depth to the stone.

The elements of living can also give persons a certain *S-age patina*. And, frankly, Lynn, I fear you may be missing out on some of it.

Lynn: I suspect you are right about that—however, I hear you saying, Darrel, that patina is not just age—it is also elements! Some of us have *aged* even longer than you, but have not been exposed to the same *elements*. No one has diagnosed me with a fatal disease—at least nothing more fatal than being seventy years old. So how do people like me move toward becoming classic, romantic aging ruins rather than just old rocks?

Darrel: Maybe it is death orientation. Augustine and Kierkegaard said we all have a fatal disease—we just have not acknowledged it yet. The enormous importance of getting in touch with our mortality is precisely my point here.

I need to tweak my previous assertion that it is impossible to conceive of our own death. Actually we can, and do, at least in some degree, conceive our own death when we consider it ironically. If Zen Buddhism can make the paradoxical statement that you climb a mountain by starting at the top, then Christianity can make a similar dramatic claim by declaring that you get your life full by facing death fully: living life from its *end*, rather than its *beginning*.

Even at the peak performance a person needs to begin letting go. Obviously this end-in-sight mentality is not easy. My patina metaphor does not call on people to quit their productive and fruitful lives. Rather, I would urge balance: run deeper, not faster. The key to holding on is letting go. Life is irony.

We're big fans of James Fowler's *Stages of Faith*.[2] Fowler appeared to be reluctant to call any of his faith stages a *better* faith (or a *bad* faith). However, I personally believe there is a better stage of faith. It is the stage where we never shirk from growing. In some ways that is my Fourth Age mission—my current ministry—to preach the gospel of *ongoing* growth. We can keep growing—if not physically, then in character, mentally and spiritually—until we take our last breathe and go to God. And one huge part of that growing is coming to real, healthy terms with our own mortality.

Stage of Faith	Task of Faithful S-Age
Infancy-Primal	Trust overcomes fears of abandonment
Intuitive-Projective	Self is differentiated from others; rituals introduced age 2-6
Mythic-Literal	Belonging most important aspect; lore learned age 7-13
Synthetic-Conventional	Personal relationship with God; generations clash age 14-18
Individuative-Reflective	Boundaries of selfhood and community clarified age 19-29
Conjunctive	Embedding of Spirit in self; God larger than symbols age 30+
Universalizing	Control surrendered to Spirit; unity of all things age 60+

Lynn: George Burns seemed to have patina. He had fun making the movies *Sunshine Boys* and *Grumpy Old Men* when he was well beyond eighty years old. Burns used to say, "Retirement at sixty-five is ridiculous. When I was sixty-five I still had pimples."

Darrel: Bully for Burns! God forbid that you ever become a Universalizing stager of faith either, Lynn—sitting on the porch, watching Texas Hill Country sunsets, and twiddling your thumbs until they cart you off to the cemetery. I want to continue to admire you as an ever-growing Conjunctive-stager.

Help Wanted

Lynn: I guess this is where I need more of your *patina.* Can you tell me—and the folks beyond the footlights—more about your own journey to this conjunctive stage?

Darrel: Well, first, I have found that the path so far is hardly linear. It is full of, at best, twists and turns that can kill our very humanity.

Lynn: Tell me about some of the twists and turns that threaten your humanity.

Thank You, Al

Darrel: Okay. For example, I hit one sharp curve when I was about thirty. I had been trying to be the perfect pastor of a large church. But inside was a poorly camouflaged anger management case. My idealism was flagging. My resentment a bonfire of vanities. A supervisor in Clinical Pastoral Education named Al one day poked around in this hornet's nest and bluntly asked, "Why are you always so angry, Darrel?" I was chagrined that my bonfire was so obvious to everyone else but me. Even my church board had seen it, I realized. A-ha! So that was why they sent me on a Continuing Pastors Education sabbatical!

I had demanded perfectionism of myself—and of others, I think. But Al did me a great service. It was the beginning of a new or emergent self. Now, years later, I can say that I know perfectibility is an illusion and it is actually, at its root, an illusion of immortality.

Remember in the movie about the *Manhattan Project* (building the first A-bomb), General Groves snaps at Dr. Robert Oppenheimer, "Quit playing God, Oppie; you're not good at it." Well I wasn't good at it either!

Reaching Upward

Lynn: You're not playing God, of course. But you do seem to be good at growing, and you've kept changing.

Darrel: For that I am thankful. I decided I did not want to be like Daniel, a character in Betty Freidan's book, who observed: "When youth is totally lost, all that is left is to be totally old."[3]

The idea is to keep adding deepening spiritual dimensions to the traditional aging factors (like health, finances, social life, and hobbies). The website of a psychologist by the name of Wong further asserts that "changing our attitudes toward aging can begin early in life and keep changing across the course of a lifetime—even at age seventy and after."[4] Lynn, meaning and purpose can creatively unfold until the end of life (even for the impaired!). And yes, even for the severely disabled.

Light Beyond the Eclipse

Lynn: For sure . . . The poet Milton wrestled with the onset of his blindness, which threatened to strip him of purpose—as his magnificent gift became useless to him. He wrote (according to one modernized version):

When I consider how my light is spent
E're half my days in this dark world and wide
And that one talent which is death to hide,
Lodged with my useless,
Though my soul more bent to serve therewith my maker
and present my true account,
lest he returning chide.
Does God exact day labor, light denied, I fondly ask.

Yet Milton finds hope and help in his final lines:

But patience, to prevent that murmur soon replied,
God does not need man's works, nor his own gifts.
They best serve God who love him best.
They also serve who only stand and wait. [5]

Milton was suggesting that we can experience authentic *meaning* and we can keep *growing*—even when we have zero capability for what is often called productive activity.

Soul Torments

Darrel: *[looking up with a wink]* Leave it to the poets to speak to the heart. Even though I am no longer equal to the hard scrabble terrain of parish ministry, which has supplied compelling purpose for most of my life, I want to believe that the quiet collaboration with you on this book is a significant part of completing my baptismal life. And your gift to me is sharing this grace.

Lynn: My apologies for the times I turn this compelling and purposeful process into a Type A pursuit of something! With your help, I am becoming more keenly aware of that streak in my nature.

In my early years I was a church planter, an all-consuming task. Added to that, I became somewhat of a young platform phenom. But I had this nagging doubt which fed a sense of failure. And I became addicted to the short-term payoffs of busy-ness and over-commitment

So much of life has been a struggle between the longing for "being versus doing"—yet fighting and vacillating between the two. *Doing* can be especially dangerous when we move so fast that the wind roars in our ears so loudly it drowns out the little voices on the inside of us that are asking big questions about *Being*.

The good news is that in these more recent years I am actually slowing the pace somewhat and I think I am listening to the little voices a bit more. My work now is more as a connector of people and a builder of a few—and a depositor of my learning into books. I really do want to exude inner peace; be a relational person who listens and encourages; the kind of person my family loves being around. I find myself moving more and more toward three simple passions:

1. To run deeper, not faster
2. To nurture primary relationships
3. To find some hands-on personal service of compassion and justice, outside the church walls and under the radar

With your help, Darrel, I am valuing my life less and less in terms of *doing* and more and more in terms of *being*.

One Great Gig

Darrel: Yes, and I think that has been happening to me in my later years, as well. Lynn, somewhere back there I began growing in my capacity to listen to people and neither judge them nor disengage from their miseries and triumphs.

I think I gradually stopped being the professional fix-it pastor. Instead, I began gradually learning the art of the player-coach-pastor.

Piled together, my thirty-six years in six parishes stack up to one great gig. That spans the spectrum of the tiny and the huge congregations—from flushing toilets to tilting at windmills with some anti-nuke-ers. Yet I honestly consider nothing I did as special. I just feel blessed to have experienced such a full range of the best and worst sides of existence.

Now having celebrated my Medicare Birthday I don't think of life so much in terms of things to accomplish, projects to complete, and goals to reach. Rather, as you know, my mantra has become, "Life is good; God is great!" Yet, I know I hold this "treasure in earthen vessels"—my life is clay well-fired but soon to be chards.[6]

Something else that has changed: In my perfectible but illusory other life, I would be ranting at God over my illness. In my new life I am speechless, but not wordless, before mystery. I can actually trace the learning curve of my maturing:

- I believed my life had a destiny.
- I came to understand how strongly I was tempted to fall into the trap of feeling useless or thinking life is pointless.
- So I grew to live with great purpose. It was not merely the best way for me to live. It was the *only* way.

Lynn: It is the only way for me too. Without an overarching sense of meaning I would surely lose my way. I think I would lose my mind!

Life as Ampersand

Darrel: I think of my life as an ampersand symbol between the bed & breakfast notation. I suggest it means more than "and." This sign had become the marker of my life. No matter what life brings my way, hope never quits. Yes, there is *this* (my present situation). But there is always *and more* . . . .

The "&" takes systemic evil into full and comprehensive account. It is not naïve to the powerful historical forces or to factors of neuroscience, DNA, or even accidental slips. Hope wrings out illusion. Hope was my kite, my rocket, my billowing cloud in the blue sky of emptiness.

The ampersand allows the distinction between life and death to stand—without illusion. Oh yes, I say again and again—and mean it more every time I say it—I am *vulnerable.* But I am also *undaunted*. These twin ideals form a refrain throughout the S-aging Drama—*vulnerable,* but *undaunted.*

Lynn: Darrel, in spite of your robust optimism and faith, at the same time just this morning I heard you speak of bone deep fatigue and pain. Can you weave your adventurous optimism together with these?

Dimming Light

Darrel: Sometimes I feel I am on a dimmer switch like the ones on our walls. The dimming for me is mostly physical. My body looks bad in the hard glare of this world. My little granddaughter looked at my face a couple of months back and asked, "Papa, what are those cracks in your face?" I have relinquished all claims to immortality—in *this world*. But my failing body generates compensating skills that free me to soar in a new space: authentic joy! No chasing the wind; no hyping of the vanities, no trying the next anti-aging scam, or even chasing off to the next generativity seminar. Feeling freed from those old enslaving and deceptive patterns, I find myself singing, "and the scenes of earth will grow strangely dim in the light of His glory and grace."[7]

I consider this a conjunctive song. It acknowledges the future without neglecting the present. A healthy ampersand.

Lynn: Darrel, you sound like my friend, Cullen Johnson, who recently succumbed after a long battle with cancer. He had retired from an executive position at Maw Bell to serve as executive director of a child placement and family counseling agency. During those final weeks before his death, Cullen suffered enormously, but with quiet dignity. For some days he had little energy even to speak, sometimes not even enough to open his eyes.

On one of these days Cullen's son Jeff sat down by his father and said, "Dad, I just want to thank you one more time for introducing me to a personal relationship with Jesus Christ." Cullen's eyes did not open, but the corners of his mouth moved up into a faint smile, and he was able to say, "He's all there is, son. *He's all there is.*"

The two sit together in long silence . . . Darrel the dying, Lynn the living-longer—maybe! Once in a while they glance into each other's faces. They both breathe long, deep breaths.

Lynn: Of course, for people of faith, death does not have the final word. As my Irish friend, Jim McQuiggin, brogues, "Ah, now, but death is highly over-rated you know."

Lynn: *[aside, poking head through the curtain]* Psst! I know it's intermission time, but it's me again. I want to say something to you about Darrel. He's not at Cullen's place of incapacity by any means. He still carries on a fairly normal routine of activities. Preaching some. Teaching a course. But he confesses that while he feels his energy slipping, his passions become more centered. When I told him about Jeff and Cullen, Darrel said, "I am moving slowly toward 'that's all there is.' There is this long dual between gravity and grace, and gravity is winning. Much of my life I have had sort of a dilettante theological appetite like a hummingbird of theology, flitting from blossom to blossom. But more and more there is only one buttercup of light and love and that's Jesus. Systematic theology may have helped me a little. But there is only one Jesus."

Sage Suggestions for a Strong Finish

How does your view of aging compare with the following statements?

- We will never get out of this world alive. Let's face it!
- Nonetheless, the goal of life is an unendingly adventurous and ever expanding one even when physical strength diminishes.
- The resulting contentment that pervades the optimistic person of faith, even at the eye of the hurricane of pain, is a marvel and a wonder. Life itself is a wonder.

Helps:

Write a paragraph or two about your observations/critique of the following quotation.

> There are four important stages in your life: You're
> born, you play for the Huskies, you get married and you die.
>
> —Dan Lynch, #58 for University of Washington Huskies of 1984.[8]

Chapter Twelve

SUB-PLOT 2—LEGACY

I met a traveler from an antique land
Who said: Two vast and trunk-less legs in stone
Stand in the desert. Near them, on the sand
Half sunk, a shattered visage lies, whose frown,
And wrinkled lip, and sneer of cold command,
Tell that its sculptor well those passions read
Which yet survive, stamped on these lifeless things.
The hand that mocked them, and the heart that fed;
And on the pedestal these words appear:
"My name is Ozymandias, king of kings:
Look on my works, ye Mighty, and despair!"
Nothing beside remains, Round the decay
Of that colossal wreck, boundless and bare
The lone and level sands stretch far away.

—Percy Bysshe Shelley [1]

"Establish the works of our hands for us, yes, establish the works of our hands."

— Psalm 90:17

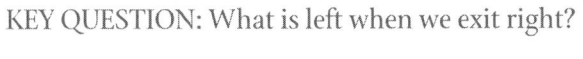

KEY QUESTION: What is left when we exit right?

Scene 12

Flashback: In the hospital, the doctor tells Barbara that Darrel's liver condition is irreversible, that he may have less than two years to live. Lynn and Darrel have walked the halls of many hospitals in their combined seven decades of ministry. Darrel is flashing back to the first numbing revelation that his condition is terminal.

Looking Down Into My Own Grave

Darrel: Shortly after my diagnosis, I felt shock waves of panic over the prospects of oblivion. One day things would be as if I had never lived. I felt like the little wave in *Tuesdays with Morrie* as it headed for the beach, anticipating oblivion when it would crash on the shores.

Lynn: *[drawing and slowly releasing a deep breath]* Whew! The thought of ceasing to exist—without leaving a trace—seems unbearable to me. I cannot imagine a person finishing strong & dying well without knowing some sense of meaningful legacy.

Darrel: You and Morrie and I are not alone in this. Scores of literary legends trace this plot: Our friend Ozymandias (at the head of this chapter) plays the tragic lead role. And Shakespeare's Macbeth also poignantly mourns "life without legacy":

> Out, out, brief candle! Life's but a walking shadow; 'Tis a poor player that struts and frets his hour upon the stage, and then is heard no more. 'Tis a tale told by an idiot, full of sound and fury, signifying nothing.[2]

Or as Sinclair Lewis said of his *Main Street* character, "He was born a man, and died a grocer."[3]

Voices of Lost Soul Legacy

Lynn: We surely don't want to go out on the bitter rubric, "Life is a bitch. And then you die." And I definitely want to leave a more significant legacy than the party-lover in the old song, "I want to live fast. Love hard. Die young. And leave a beautiful memory."

Darrel: Indeed, the words "lost souls" comes to mind here. I don't mean souls hell bent and anxious to be saved, but lost souls in the sense of their pitiable condition. Tiny wandering stars disappearing in the blackness of outer space.

These wander everywhere—uprooted, alienated, despairing—and most give little thought to what they will leave on stage when they exit. Seems they have missed the piece of the plot called *Legacy*.

The ancient Hebrew poet wrote, "Establish the works of our hands for us. Yes establish the works of our hands."[4] Was he longing to leave a legacy?

What Kind of Legacy?

Darrel: But to make sure we don't miss it ourselves, we must ask, In healthy S-aging terms, what in fact is an authentic and valid legacy? Lynn, what does it mean to you personally?

Lynn: Ah! Great question, Darrel. Is it a face on Mount Rushmore? Or your byline on a book? A Fortune 500 company named after me? Or maybe a life-saving vaccine named after you? Or even a string of successful relationships? A spiritual renewal movement? A healthy family system? Just what *is* worth leaving behind when we die?

Darrel: Some people actually write their own obituaries, as though they could determine their legacy! That is a lost cause. From a human perspective our accomplishments—and even we ourselves—are quite quickly forgotten, often even long before we die. As ancient scripture says, "There is no remembrance of men of old, and even those who are yet to come will not be remembered by those who follow."[5]

Lynn: For sure. This hit me in the face on a recent visit to a large church where Carolyn and I served for nearly twenty years. I walked into the familiar offices, whistling and waiting to see heads pop out office doors to greet me. But—would you believe—I had to check out several different offices before anyone knew me! For a bit there, this made me question how effective that twenty year ministry was.

Success or Significance?

Darrel: What you are saying echoes Bob Buford's second half in his book *Half Time.* In his mid to late forties, as Buford puts it, the focus of his life shifted from success to *significance.*

This seems to parallel the Philosopher Sage of Ecclesiastes whose newfound wisdom has put him on the significance track. In fact, it seems that both Buford and the Philosopher Sage of Ecclesiastes have discovered a new self that is no longer stuck in the early adult stages. They have experienced that fundamental re-orientation or breakthrough toward meaningful legacy.[6]

Lynn: I think one of those breakthroughs was triggered for me by an emergency room episode last January. Since I launched Hope Network Ministries[7] nine years ago, my life became the busiest ever. Sometimes I was so over-committed that my focus had shrunk to just keeping the pace. But when I woke up in ER and found out that my family thought I had nearly died, I certainly did some major life assessment. During my brief hospital stay, my kids and grandkids gathered around me and reminded me that at the end of the day, these relationships are infinitely more significant than anything I might accomplish through my over-committed lifestyle.

Caving In?

Darrel: You know I have been concerned about your pace. But I wouldn't want to see you go to the other extreme either—to just quit and vegetate and leave no significant legacy. That is what I sometimes fear for myself—*inertia!* I am haunted by the way my own brother seemed arrested in the stagnation of Middle and Late Adulthood. He seemed unable to be caring and giving. He suffered a terrible narcissism and, at the end of life, appeared to withdraw into his cave.

On my worst days I battle the temptation to stop growing. Growth demands change—and I resist the discomfort of change. My present misery is comfortable because at least it is the enemy that I know.

Transcen-Dance

Darrel: Joan Erikson's point in *The Life Cycle Completed* is precisely that such despair, bitterness, and withdrawal are the great enemies of generativity.[8] For the polar opposite to withdrawal, Joan Erikson adds the elegant word gerotranscen-*dance* (sic, Erikson deliberately mispells) which is also a choice open in the ninth stage. She exclaims: "Transcen-dance—that's it, of course! And it moves.

It's one of the arts, it's alive, sings, and makes music, and I hug myself because of the truth it whispers to my soul."[9]

I want this dance—the transcen-dance—to become my own choreography. Not with machismo or bravado, but as a human fully capable of living with the thought of my own death, confident of meaningful legacy.

Again, I am not alone. I may even be the norm. For example, Zorba the Greek will always be remembered more for his dance than for his folly.

Family Legacy

Darrel: And when it comes to loving others and savoring daily life, I guess *family* heads my legacy wish list. The ancient Hebrew people saw children and children's children as legacy—and even more. Even as eternal life—life extended after death through the lives of descendents.

So, what does legacy look like as you envision it, Lynn?

Lynn: Well, Big D, family tops my legacy list too. And my ideal family legacy includes at least two features: *memories* and *character*.

Memories? That my kids and grandkids will remember me not so much as a writer, a minister, a leader—but far more as a connected, and attentive, and loving husband-father-grandfather presence. Someone they enjoyed being around and trusted with everything in them.

Character? I dream of leaving my offspring with vibrant faith and sterling values. Early in our parenting career Carolyn and I actually set parental goals. We wanted our children to . . .

. . . own a vibrant faith

. . . nurture healthy relationships

. . . be self-starters

. . . own healthy self esteem

. . . be loving, hospitable, servant-hearted persons who make a positive difference

Of course, only time and the testimony of others will tell if this is really the family legacy we leave. But at least it is what we aimed for.

Beyond Family

Darrel: So a valued legacy would be left through family. But is there another legacy you want to leave behind?

Lynn: I will answer yes, but with a caveat: that part of legacy is a bit more amorphous. A friend, Max Lucado, sat next to a German businessman at a dinner. To make conversation, Max asked the European what kind of business he was in. The German replied, "I am a Keeper of the Forest." Max probed further, "And what does a 'keeper of the forest' do?" The businessman explained, "Well, in simple terms: I harvest the trees my father planted. And I plant the trees my sons will harvest."

Keeper of the Forest is a metaphor for another piece of my envisioned legacy. As John Maxwell says, "A success without a successor is a failure." In my S-aging years I feel a passion to distill the best of what life has taught me, and pass it on to at least a few persons in the next generation. And train them to pass it on to others after them. My writing is part of that, I think. So is Hope Network Ministries, the para-church ministry I lead. Our mission statement is *to coach and mentor visionary Christian leaders and equip them with the heart and skills to lead effectively in a twenty-first century environment.*

Darrel, you have hinted that it is never too late to change the dream of what we want our legacy to look like. And it seems to me that that since your diagnosis, legacy must have come into much sharper focus for you.

So beyond family as legacy, what legacy do you want to leave?

Darrel Ponders His Legacy

Darrel: In the mode of Paul Harvey, I have imagined Gilbertson's fictional "rest of the story" ending to the Book of Ecclesiastes. Of course we don't know how old our Sage is at the time of his writing. In my epiphany version he is sixty years old. He still has time to transform the vanity of his lifeless boredom into vibrant living. He is morphing himself into an intentional mentor & giver instead of the receiver & getter, savoring daily life and sharing from his considerable reserve of gifts. He is now my poster boy for significant legacy.

What follows is part of my "rest of the story." That is, an additional chapter I have written to help the writer of Ecclesiastes clarify himself *[winks and grins]*:

> 8. One day as I was strolling in my garden, I heard the gardener singing an uncommonly happy song. 9. I asked if he was as happy as he seemed. 10. His response, like a voice from beyond, was, "I am always happy when I am giving myself away." 11. I was thunderstruck. Could this be the secret? Could this be the key to the mystery door of life's deepest meaning? 12. I immediately turned my mind to a simple plan. 13. First I surveyed my assets and skills. Then I devised a scheme to use these as gifts—for *my own* learning and living. 14. But soon, astonished at my foolishness, I again asked the gardener how he made the place so beautiful. 15. He detailed his love for plants, and his mastery of gardening and I saw that his happiness was in serving *others*. 16. I began to see the gardener as a metaphor for my new life chapter: *significance*. 17. The last half of life is not a time of acquiring, but a time of releasing, of letting go.

Like the Philosopher Sage in Ecclesiastes, I want to be remembered as one who gave himself away—and yet lived life to the last breath and loved every moment of it, warts and all. From whom family and friends take comfort—and may even be inspired to attempt the same.

Lynn: I think I hear you fine-tuning the significance idea. Not long ago a friend said, "The search for significance is *idolatry*!" Stunned me a bit. Yet, it is true that our need for doing or being something significant could be self-centered, ego-driven. Or as another friend put it, "Can you explain the difference between 'focus on leaving a legacy' and a man who tries to 'save his own life?'" A good question in the light of what Jesus said, "Whoever wants to save his life, will lose it. But whoever loses his life for me will find it."[10] Why not just consistently live true to your calling and values and the legacy (good or bad) will be left, whether you will it or not?

Darrel: To approach the heart of significant legacy we must mature past self-preoccupation into a heartfelt lifestyle of sharing and serving.

Lynn: Looks to me like you are good at it. And your family concurs. When I asked your son Todd, "What is the best legacy your father will leave you?" he answered, "Loving service. Dad left a string of churches a lot better than he found them. He earned the highest title *Doctor,* but much preferred *Pastor*—because his calling was to be a self-giving servant and loving husband and father."

Faith as Legacy

Darrel: Now that is reassuring—and a little embarrassing. But I would add one thing more: *Faith*. I discern meaningful legacy through a faith lens. Remember, the Bible says, "Unless the LORD builds the house, its builders labor in vain."[11]

Faith *is* the Cradle of my Certainty. Let me wax eloquent a moment. I declare I am a Christ-bearing cipher. Having suffered the fires of this world's furnace of doubt and deep wounds of angst, I defiantly rise to a new life in a happy vision of joy and wonder. To God be highest praise.

Lynn: Whew! Grand vision, Pastor Gilbertson—like lines from one of your finer sermons. Seems like we are peering through the same lens. I too am a believer in a mysterious and inexplicable God who is master of life at its best, and whose ideal we look toward for human wholeness and community health. He is our legacy!

Darrel: Yes, Lynn, over the last six years, I have come to understand that though death may come to me like Morrie's little wave crashing on shore and into oblivion . . . fearing the end of all things, the little wave shouts to another wave behind it for help. The other wave yells "not to worry." We do not disappear but we are all taken back up into the great ocean again and our life goes on. Legacy! That speaks of my solidarity with humanity—and of "life with God"—not my puny individuality.

Lynn: I think Whittier said it well for both of us:

> We search the world for good, we cull
> The bright, the great, the beautiful

And weary seekers of the best,
    We come home laden from our quest
And find that all the sages said,
    Was in the book our Fathers read?"

Darrel: And St. Augustine said, "We are made for you, O God, and Restless are our souls until they rest in you."

So the curtain falls and hush fills the theater.

Sage Suggestions for a Strong Finish

How would you modify or comment upon these statements:

- We all long for significant legacy.
- You will be remembered one way or the other.
- The way you would like to be remembered is your generativity project for the last half of your life.
- Issues of the *heart* will be treasured long after issues of the *head.*
- What *you are* matters for more than what *you accomplish.*

Helps

To enrich the dimensions of your legacy you can do the following

1. Write a paragraph describing the daimon or primary motivating force/driver in your life. For clues, check the trail of evidence from your life's vocation, interests, and even hobbies.
2. Now write a paragraph in the form of a commentary for television entitled, THE BIG STORY. Include WHO, WHAT, WHEN and WHERE along with the HOW of your life.
3. After you have the headline story, spell out what is left undone in your life. What are the unfinished tasks, the stillborn dreams and the unfulfilled yearnings?

4. Get started on the “rest of your legacy” TO DO list today:

Chapter Thirteen

SUB-PLOT 3—IDENTITY

> "I went into the woods because I wished to live deliberately, to confront only the essential facts of life, and to see if I could not learn what it had to teach and not, when I came to die, discover I had not lived."
>
> —THOREAU

KEY QUESTION: Who are you really? Honestly? And without sham?

Scene 13

In Darrel's study two analog gentleman are trying to read the digital LCD screen. Lynn peers over Darrel's shoulder, as Darrel points at the headline on the web page: Identity theft.

Darrel: Tammy, our oldest daughter, discovered identity theft the hard way: standing in a checkout line—people in line leering—her credit card was rejected because a thief had maxed it out. She felt humiliated. She felt helpless too, as it took months to correct accounts, and retrieve her identity from the black hole of cyberspace.

I'll bet she felt morally outraged. But the truth is, she didn't really lose her *identity!* Tammy is still who she is. No one can take that away from her. What is our identity? How would you define yourself? What is Darrel's *identity*?

What Really is Identity?

Darrel: Now, there's a tough question. But I'll give it a try. After all, one would think that living sixty-eight years has helped me get some kind of handle on my self-hood. Self-understanding takes time . . . ages I believe.

He pointed to a chart of the Four Ages. (See page 45.)

The *First Age* establishes the baseline of self—or core identity. In my First Age my mother lamented, "Either Darrel will grow up to be the Pope or Al Capone." Since I was a Lutheran, Pope was out, but my willfulness suggested Capone might be in the running.

I think most of one's self-understanding takes place in the first twenty to twenty-five years of life. In those years, my chief aim was to control my own destiny. Athletics was a positive outlet for this energy—and high-school basketball also taught me some discipline. In college, I poured this energy and discipline into academics—and excelled. But not at first and not without a cost.

Know Thyself

Darrel: Just because my Inner Self was emerging into some sort of external persona did not mean I *understood* that Self. In fact, I consider myself a slow learner. That may have been because, although I was disciplined, I had not learned how to apply discipline to study. One professor rankled me by returning a paper with the words—"DIG, DIG, DIG." (He did not know that these were my initials!) He was right, though—and my learning picked up pace and moved deeper than the surface.

My Second Age (twenty five years to fifty years of age) was turbulent as I headed into an identity crisis.

Then I sort of zipped through my Third Age which lasted only a decade (about fifty to sixty years of age). Looking back from what is currently my Fourth Age (the last eight years of my life), I likely have as complete a Self-understanding as I probably will gain.

Elemental Life

Lynn: Two basic drives are at tension as every human being searches for identity. One is the drive to merge with a community and the other is the drive to stand out from that community. These two drives are in conflict, and the measure of resolution one finds for the conflict provides the degree of peace or stability of a person's inner life. Has this resolution of the tension between drives to merge and drives to stand out at least partly clarified your identity?

Darrel: I was in a furious struggle to find this resolution. On one hand, I was a pastor, a socially approved role. On the other hand, I also wanted to be an iconoclast, different or unique—somewhat of a prophet-to-community. I would almost describe this collision as the battle for my soul. Possibly soul and identity amount to much the same thing.

One vivid example of this collision was when my personal conscience led me to protest the Vietnam war, resulting in the public consequence of being vilified by many in my own congregation, and mocked by the larger community.

It was also during this time that I began to feel the painful limits of my ability to control my life. I have always had this strange sense that my mother may have whispered into my ear as I slept in my crib, "You have a destiny." Although I am not sure to this day what that destiny might have been. I am sure, however, that whatever my destiny, I usually did not control it. By the time I was thirty-five years of age I had to admit to myself that I could not change the world, or even change my Self! I guess I was coming-of-age.

Darrel: *[sliding another sheet of paper toward Lynn]* The spiritual and moral implications of this part of the journey are spelled out in this chart called the Bi-columnar of Human Development. It compares Erikson and Fowler, helping nuance the S-aging journey.[1]

Bi-Columnar on Human Development

Chronology	Erikson (Psycho-social Stages)	Fowler (Spiritual-moral Stages)
Stage 1—1 to 2	Infancy Trust v. Mistrust/Hope	Primal—Fundamental trust
Stage 2—2	Autonomy v. Doubt/ Will	None
Stage 3—Pre-school	Initiative v. Guilt/ Purpose	Intuitive-Projective—Differentiating Self/ Other
Stage 4—Early School	Industry v. Inferiority/ Competence	Mythic-Literal—Belonging to one's Family
Stage 5—Adolescence	Identity v. Confusion/Fidelity	Synthetic-Conventional—Values clash w/ Family
Stage 6—Young Adult	Intimacy v. Isolation/ Love	Individuative-Reflective—Boundary Clarification
Stage 7—Middle Adult	Generativity v. Stagnation/ Caring	Conjunctive—God greater than symbols/ spirituality
Stage 8—Late Adulthood	Integrity v. Despair/ Wisdom	Universalizing—No longer self-referen-tial/Spirit led
Stage 9—Elderhood (Darrel's term)	Withdrawal v. Gerotranscen-dance (Joan Erikson's term]	None

Faith Development

Lynn: This chart helps me get a better handle on Erikson. Could you coach me a bit on Fowler's Faith Stages?[2]

Stages and Tasks of Faith

Stage of Faith	Task of Faithful Age
Primal Trust overcomes fears of abandonment	Infancy
Intuitive-Projective	Self is differentiated from others; rituals introduced 2-6
Mythic-Literal	Belonging most important aspect; lore learned 7-13
Synthetic-Conventional	Personal relationship with God; generations clash 14-18
Individuative-Reflective	Boundaries of selfhood and community clarified 19-29
Conjunctive	Embedding of Spirit in self; God larger than symbols 30+
Universalizing	Control surrendered to Spirit; unity of all things 60+

Lynn: These developmental ideas are pretty fascinating stuff. But it is complicated and abstract. So Darrel—here we go again—help me connect this theory to your own personal experience.

Darrel: I'll try. At thirty-five, when I protested the Vietnam War, I struggled between my internal conviction versus my external role. I was moving further along in my ever-changing identity or Self-understanding. I was beginning to develop my own set of values and, at least within my family relationships, to shape these into a consistent form and practice.

Actually, the importance of Knowing Self goes back to the Old Testament book of Proverbs as well as to the Greek philosophers. Shakespeare put this notion into the famous beautiful soliloquy:

> This above all: *to thine own self be true.*
> And it must follow, as the night the day,
> Thou canst not then be false to any man.[3]

Darrel's Third Age

Darrel: The daylight further dawned upon me, as serious health problems began even as early as age thirty-five. Three more hit me in my fifties. And now in my sixties the fourth major health issue described as fatal. Now there is no denying I am vulnerable, finite, mortal—and dying. My idealistic and invincible world has come crashing down. However, in the process I have been continually discovering more of who I really am. And, of course, that I am surely not in control of my destiny. Someone else is.

Enter the power of faith. There is good news. Really good news.

Best of all, the object of that faith with which I have come to reckon (unlike my tyrannical former false gods—athleticism or academics or world changer) is a God of grace. This God forgives and renews me. My inner strength mounts up on the wings of an eagle, to borrow the poetry of Isaiah.

Lynn: But I often hear you speak of dangerous or tantalizing detours and seismic disruptions in the path of finishing strong & dying well. Where do these fit into the flight of an eagle?

Double Demons

Darrel: Two demons. My first is *risk aversion.*

Peter Drucker, the business guru, says there are four kinds of risks.

1. The risk you *must accept*
2. The risk you *can* afford to take
3. The risk you *cannot* afford to take
4. The risk you cannot afford *not* to take.[4]

When I accepted a job in Texas, my mother, who had spent her whole life in Wisconsin, asked, “Why would you want to leave the Midwest?” To me it was a risk I could not afford *not* to take. Several months earlier I had stood in the winter’s bleak parsonage window listening (on one of those old 78 LPs) to Glen Campbell sing “Galveston”— a song about a Spanish-American War soldier pining for a lover who was back on the Texas coast. He was lonely—and looking back. However, for me the song was a vision of what might yet be—looking ahead. So I took the risk—pulled up stakes and headed to Texas. I believe taking that risk also took me a giant step toward mature self-understanding.

Risk aversion comes in several forms but always represents a serious detour from our path to maturity.

Lynn: And the second demon?

Darrel: *Freeze-framing.* The altogether too common illusion that one can stop history, or at least delay one’s flow with history, long enough to finish one’s own puny plan.

One of my favorite people is a North Dakota wheat farmer named Walter. As his pastor I stood in Walter’s machine shed one afternoon after a tremendous hail storm ripped through his wheat fields and wiped out a whole season’s crop. After the storm a spectacular rainbow appeared and Walter announced, “Well, pastor, I don’t know about you but I am going to grab a bucket, gather up some ice, and crank us some ice cream!”

I bask in Walter’s indomitable hope. He could not stop time or the elements so he courageously, and positively, chose to go with the flow of history.

Bravo Walter! You refused to freeze-frame!

“Vanity of vanities. All is vanity and a striving after the wind.”[5] The movie *Gone With the Wind* got its name from these words from Ecclesiastes. The South, though defeated, still clung to its vision of the past (trying to freeze frame antibellum time.) The Philosopher Sage of Ecclesiastes would call this a “chasing after the wind.” History will not be stopped. I call these attempts denial mechanisms: the vain delusion of attempting to make permanent what is only temporary.

Risk aversion or *freeze-framing*—either one of these devious traps threatens to impede forward-progress on the S-aging journey.

A Totally Amazing but *Un*-Remarkable Fourth Age

Darrel: I was discovering (and as well being captured by) the idea that my Self could continually grow, change and evolve. I never strayed far from that pathway since. But the shattering fault line—the sure and certain vision of my own death—even more sharply defined that course.

From somewhere I mustered the courage to follow the course some call integrity, though I prefer to call it *character*. Character is a multi-layered and nuanced enhancement of integrity. The stuff of whistle blowers—resolute and resilient in the face of threat.

Life-Long Learning Curve

Lynn: In other words, *S-aging* is not merely aging, correct? Nor does *S-aging* imply a completed achievement. Rather, I hear you saying it is a chosen course we follow. Identity shaping—the growth of integrity or of character—is a life-long learning curve, as our Self-understanding keeps morphing and expanding to journey's end. S-aging is the adventure of living out life to its end, all the way.

Darrel: *[chuckling and again tweaking Lynn's ideas]* Well, maybe something like ninety percent of S-aging is journey and maybe ten percent is goal. But there is a goal. Did you hear about the parishioner who told the pastor that when she died she wanted to be placed in the casket with a fork in her hand? When the pastor asked why, she explained, "Because I've always been told to keep the fork when the dirty dishes are picked up at the church potluck—you don't want to miss the dessert. *THE BEST IS YET TO COME!"*

Lynn, in spite of being fully aware of my fatal illness, my *FOURTH AGE IDENTITY IS THE BEST YET.*

Sage Suggestions for a Strong Finish

Some questions to ponder

1. Why is there no S-aging without out the hard work of *Self*-understanding?
2. Why is there no continuous growth in Self-hood without honest reflection and serious application of lessons learned? Give some examples from your own life.
3. Comment on this quote: "The destination (or destiny) is not the point; the joy and adventure of life lived fully on the road as a pilgrim (and not a tourist) is the point of S-aging."

Powerline

Identity is each person's ever changing and renewable inner life task we call the Self-hood.

Helps

The authors propose that S-aging is often used as a noun, but is in real life a verb? Write a sentence or two on how you understand this claim.

Now write a brief essay on your own view of the end of life and how it will make all the difference in how you live the last Ages of your life____________

____

REVIEWS

Critics Corner

Chapter Fourteen

ENCORE: THE PLAYERS LOOK BACK

"The last of human freedoms is the ability to choose our attitude, no matter the circumstances."

—VICTOR FRANKL

"Do you know how hard it is to find a real sympathy card? There is so much 'bad theology' at Hallmark!"

—BARBARA GILBERTSON

KEY QUESTION: What did the players/directors learn from this journey?

Scene 14

Darrel says his energy level isn't what it was five years ago. Emerging from his somnolent refresher, he has an idea that both men could do a Butler-esque life review,[1] *a personal reflection on the inter-play between the three life-strands: internal developments, career paths—and S-aging.*

Darrel: What do you think? Should we do a life review?

Lynn: Sounds great.

Darrel: You first!

Lynn Looks Back

Lynn: My ministry began differently from most, I think. Actually, through the last year and a half of high school, I was making talks almost every Sunday mostly at small rural churches. Kind souls there graciously called those talks preaching—which of course also fed my ego. Formal training, however, began at a Christian liberal arts college, where I majored in Communications and minored in Biblical Studies. I also did supply preaching on weekends. So I have preached somewhere almost every Sunday since my freshman year in college!

It would be a stretch to call all of it preaching or even ministry—but it was a start.

By the summer of my college junior year I had begun speaking in rural southern revivals. Some of these ran eight or ten nights. And since I had only a handful of talks in my repertoire, I had little choice but to hit the floor and the books around 5 A.M. most mornings—cramming to stay ahead of the crowds.

Faith Crisis

Lynn: After marrying and a year of graduate seminary, Carolyn and I moved to British Columbia, Canada, to help start a new church in the village of Salmon Arm. Carolyn was pregnant and we had a two year old in tow. We were nine hundred miles from nearest kin and way in over our heads. That church is still there. But those four years brought my first major faith and ego crisis to a head, and for a time I think I was—secretly of course—almost agnostic.

This crisis, in part, prompted me to leave that church and return to further graduate studies, hoping—among other things—to resolve the faith crisis. The faith crisis did resolve, somewhat, with exposure to a healthier theology. But that raised a new challenge: how to fit my significantly altered theological perspective into the framework of my denomination—which I loved and still love very much.

But we returned to British Columbia with a fresh message to help start another church, in Kelowna, staying five years.

However, those years led me to yet another crossroads. I had become a somewhat visible young platform speaker within my fellowship, and discovered that the things I did best didn't fit in domestic missions. That was the positive side. However, it took me a while to begin facing the fact that a lethal combination of a distorted sense of calling, mixed in with a highly volatile dose of narcissism, had put my little church—and far more importantly, my little family—in jeopardy.

Transitions

Lynn: Then I was called—providentially both Carolyn and I still believe—to a large established church in the United States Bible Belt—something this Canadian country boy would never have imagined himself doing. This new context offered two very much needed ingredients: first, a better fit theologically and for my skill set and passions, and second, the much needed structure and accountability of wise elders and a multiple staff.

In the years since that move, my career path (though I find it rather distasteful to refer to ministry as a career) has led to an ever broadening scope of ministry. First to *teaching*: for many years I have taught one graduate university course a year as an adjunct professor. Second, *writing*: the last two decades, I have contributed regularly to several journals and have written nine books. Third, *leadership development*: the last decade my career has morphed into leadership development in a para-church organization, though a part of me will always miss local congregational ministry.

However, through all these years a part of me which longed for internal depth and a measured pace constantly warred with another part of me: drivenness and a tendency to overcommit. Frankly, I must admit that I have almost habitually let the sheer busy-ness of it all interfere with much needed and much longed for introspection.

The big surprise has been that our friendship has helped lead me to far more seriously explore my own inner journey. While I thought at first our joint writing project would be a sort of *Tuesdays with Morrie* journal of *your journey*, it has turned out to be a book of substance representing *our journey together*.

The last few years have brought an exciting new learning curve. Frankly, our book project has forced me into some terrain I may never have had the wisdom or the courage to explore on my own. It has also sharply raised my awareness of the vanity denial—and gotten me more intentionally peeling the layers off the onion of who I am and what these later stages of life are doing in me. And, much as I don't like to admit it, Darrel, you are helping me come to terms with my tendency toward over commitment and to track down the issues that drive it. Whether intentional or not, you are helping me re-examine my life priorities and in many other ways have led me to be immersed in the S-aging journey. I think I am actually learning the richness that comes with moving at a measured pace.

I have watched and listened—through our conversations and emails—and picked up on your progression through the stages of dealing with finishing strong & making plans to die well. Your journey has, in many respects, become my journey. Yes, I have a long way to go—but I really do believe that I am now on the S-Aging journey.

Darrel Looks Back

Darrel: *[Reflecting on Lynn's story with a final nod and smile]* Guess it's my turn now.

As you and I have been though this writing project—playing our roles in this drama—I have done a lot of grieving. But I have also learned many valuable lessons. Two great learnings stand out above the rest.

First, I too have learned the richness of moving at a measured pace. All my life I have been in a hurry. My parents noted this early on. They found it charming. But I see lopsidedness. Most of my life I was told to slow down.

My case of the hurries first showed up on the Wisconsin farm. As a lad of six years I could not wait to do my chores and ran hopping on one foot while I tied my other shoelace.

Later I became a confirmed sooner (not an Oklahoman but a sooner as opposed to a later) in study habits. Dreading late rushes to deadlines, I would be a week early in my preparation and writing.

But that is only part of the picture. Hurry also meant efficiency. Wasted time in my dressing and morning toilet habits was such a frustration that I found faster decision-making, laying out my clothes the night before, and simpler methods, two things at a time if possible—shaving and showering.

Throughout my whole career I always rose earlier than anyone—to jog or walk, and then to be in the office to get a morning's worth of work done before the other workers arrived. Productivity peeked by 8 A.M.! Even now, late in life, I love to wake to the gurgling of a coffee pot set on automatic and having set out breakfast ingredients the night before.

If all of this seems neurotic—of course it is. Compulsive too. But the good news is that I am learning to relax in the luxury of retirement and to move through my days at, as you say, a more measured pace. Those waiting lines at the checkout stand or the traffic light that once set my knee to jiggling are now welcome times to just be. Unwanted early retirement has turned out to be a gift.

The Death Hurries

Darrel: Then I got a case of the death hurries. So what is the big thrill in the big chill? Most of us consider the real shocker in death is its timing (or its ill-timing). But a second lesson I have learned came as an even greater shock: though I am dying, I am still growing and living vitally.

This process has also exposed my own age-istic mentality. Like most men I thought of aging as some sort of a dual lessening project: dementia and *Depends*! What a shock when I discovered an autumnal surging, an Indian summer during my dying. I am now *more* than I ever was—with all the physical compensations and volatile circumstances of my health. I am more whole, more integrative, more able to put together the pieces of the puzzle.

When I think about my life I surprise myself. I am at peace within, of course. I will eventually—maybe soon—fall into frail or terminal un-health, but in the meantime, aging is positively great. This is the best time of my life!

Shared Learnings

What follows are additional things we've learned together through our journey.

Of course every person is unique, as is every third stage of life—and every death. Yet together we are finding some significant, and near universal, common threads.

First, together *we are learning that we human beings almost universally struggle to honestly face our mortality and our dying*. We all face the dangerous temptation of denial. But at the same time humankind all have the power of choice, the option of intentionality—*carpe deum*—to seize the moment.

Second, *we are learning that life unfolds in fairly predictable ages or stages*—each with its own unique Life Track.

Third, we are also *learning that it is much healthier to walk out into the middle of our mortality and poke around in it,* rather than to distance ourselves from the thought of it by means of all sorts of denial mechanisms.

Fourth, we *are definitely learning that with thoughtful S-aging life can become ever more richly textured,* its meaning increasingly more layered and nuanced in the years down near the finish line and can be lived to the full—till our chests hit the ribbon.

Finally, possibly the *most important thing we are learning is the necessity of the other*—that one plus one equals far more than two, that we do our S-aging, our strongest finishing, and our best dying in the long company of authentic friends.

SAGE SUGGESTIONS FOR A STRONG FINISH

POWERLINE

"I'm convinced that what we keep owns us, and what we give away sets us free"
—Rev. Martin Luther Agnew Jr.[2]

HELPS

A Tool for Memoir Writing

This is a pump primer to get you started on your story. The most important parts are your defining events/experiences, your *self-definition* and your *spiritual journey*.

- What is your claim to fame (interesting trivia about you)?
- Birth place and date.
- Parents—including vocation and faith. Siblings.
- Schooling—chronologically, and your current vocation.
- *Define yourself—what kind of person am I?*
- If married tell how you met your spouse and her faith. (Children if any).
- *Sketch your spiritual journey:* The highest point, the lowest point. Your chronic struggle. Your sweet spot. What you want next.
- What events/experiences shaped you, define you.
- In what service projects are you currently involved either as a volunteer or as paid staff?
- If money were no object, what would you do with the next ten years of your life?
- What is your all-consuming passion?

Chapter Fifteen

A CAST OF REAL LIFE CHARACTERS

Some real life stories of finishing strong & dying well.

KEY QUESTION: How did some friends of the authors finish strong & die well?

Lynn: During out conversations, Darrel, you have triggered so many great ideas. One of your best was the day you said, "Let's leave the readers with some real faces." Fabulous notion. We have both loved and lost some great human spirits along the way. And admired others from afar. Let's swap some cameo shots of real life players, who are finishing strong or who died well. Why don't you kick things off?"

GAZ GREEN

Darrel: OK Lynn, I'll start with my friend, Gaz Green. It was Gaz's last time in a semi-official capacity as one of the key supporters behind our local symphony series, and a day we honored him. Gaz had trouble walking on stage. But finally there he stood, surrounded by a cast of co-leaders, looking out on a full concert hall of admirers. It was his day.

When Gaz finally spoke, he was, as always, gracious and generous to a fault. Everyone else got the credit for what he had started and nurtured. But the folks in that packed hall all knew better. Someone said he must be "the world's best public relations man." Across a lifetime with Procter and Gamble and Coca-Cola, he had matched people and talent with seamless charm and effectiveness.

Now his remarks came to a conclusion. "Finally," he announced (he is more than eighty years old), "I want to tell you about my vision for the symphony." Tears welled in my eyes. He shared his vision. In a few deft sentences, he portrayed a forward leaning picture for the organization. It was magical to me. This was the way to leave a group one has served—and to exit the stage of life.

Gaz is definitely finishing strong!

Don Bowen

Lynn: One of the special persons taking the stage in my memory is Don Bowen. Don played football in college. He married his college sweetheart and they had two children. After law school Don became one of the top mediation specialists in the country.

When his marriage died, Don was determined to learn from the failure and move his life to a higher plain. Although he became a nationally visible attorney, with a lucrative practice (*Fortune* Magazine named him one of the top ten attorneys in the country), he never forgot the less fortunate. Time and again, Don quietly gave his legal expertise—gratis—to good people who fell on bad times. One example was a Hispanic family who worked for years building their mom and pop Mexican food operation. Then a national franchise took the same name the mom and pop store had used from day one. The franchise sued the local people and would have run them out of business had Don not taken the case and saved their mom and pop store—free and anonymously. Multiple such stories could be told.

Don remarried, had another son, and never forgot his roots. His father was a rancher and an artist. Don inherited a passion for the ranch country and his own brand of artistic flair. He built a house on the high ridge looking across vast ranchlands.

Then at the height of his career (but at a young age) pancreatic cancer took Don down. Though he fought valiantly and prayed hard, Don also honestly and calmly faced the inevitable. He continued to practice law till the end, determined to complete some important cases, so as not to let vulnerable people down. Just days before he died, Don addressed the Texas Bar Association, told them he was dying with peace and confidence. He testified to his faith in God and encouraged his peers and colleagues.

With his final energy, Don planned his own funeral, and hired a man to build the plain box that was to be his casket.

Don died at home. Next morning, the family rose early, placed Don's body in the plain box and, in the dawning light, took him out to his beloved west Texas ranch and buried him beneath the soil he loved to roam. My friend Don finished strong and died well.

Jim Wacker

Darrel: We have known some pretty noble souls, haven't we, Lynn? Coach Jim Wacker was another one of these.

Jim's gargantuan funeral was national news and thousands of persons voiced their appreciation for him. Wacker had touched many people deeply and made a singular impact on the world of sports. Coach Wacker's integrity was legend, and his enthusiasm for life unbounded. And his love for the game of football as a vehicle for building young men was unmatched.

But he did not lead a life of charmed luck; nor was his sunny view of life Pollyanna-ish. His story is also one of the thrill of victory and the agony of defeat. He coached national champions; but was also fired from a Big Ten university position. Life came to him in all its nobility—and its unpleasantness. Yet Jim defiantly refused to be beaten down.

So what was the key to his life? Before his death he told his pastor to remind those who came to his funeral that his priorities had always been the same and listed them:

faith
family
friends . . . and
FOOTBALL

His view was longitudinal, pointing to the end of all things (including death), rather than being caught up in the present. His method was utmost respect for everyone he met or coached. Jim never met a person in whom he did not see potential.

One person that Jim had let go from his program called during Wacker's last days in hospice, with praise and love for his old coach. "He loved me," said the young and difficult student athlete. Coach Jim had cut this person from the team, but in doing so had let the young man keep his scholarship and get his education.

Jim was like that—the everlasting encourager. People who called him in those last days to cheer up Jim, usually hung up being cheered by him.

I have often said, "I want to die in Texas; and I want to die like Jim Wacker!"

Carolyn Salmon

Lynn: Darrel, you've likely never heard of a tall red-headed lady named Carolyn Salmon, but she was almost a legend in the city of Abilene, Texas. She married young, to an aspiring minister. Still young, they moved to Long Island, New York, to serve in an exciting urban mission project. By the time they had been there eight years, the couple had six children. Then the wheels came off their marriage. Carolyn met betrayal and abandonment.

After the divorce, Carolyn lay in bed grieving for two weeks—feeling devastated and victimized, unable to function. Then, suddenly, "the victim disappeared and a lioness emerged, with a steel will and a passion to protect and care for her cubs," as her son described it.

She moved the family back to Texas to be near family, friends, and a very supportive church, and taught school to make ends meet. She made life fun. Her children tell of her non-judgmental love and her reverence for God. Carolyn raised them each to be creative and unique.

Carolyn overcame further betrayal by more than one "religious man" and she suffered enormously with health problems, but never surrendered and never complained.

After her kids grew up, Carolyn traveled with friends. When she was found dead in her modest home, she had already bought tickets for her next trip. She died with a peaceful expression on her face, simply falling asleep.

At her funeral, Carolyn's children told fascinating tales of how she always made life fun. One was of a policeman stopping Carolyn for speeding, just after she has spilled a cup of coffee on the lap of her white pantsuit. The trooper swaggered up to her window asking, "What is your hurry, ma'am?"

"Oh, you scared me so bad," Carolyn said, pointing to her lap. "Look what happened." The policeman turned and fled to his patrol car, while the kids giggled in the backseat.

Another time, an unwanted suitor came calling. Carolyn stayed in a back room. The kids had cut eyeholes in bed sheets and dressed up as ghosts—they circled the poor man, shouting "Woo hoo!" until he picked up his hat and left.

This kind of fun and creativity still swirled around Carolyn until the day she fell into that final sleep. Carolyn Salmon finished strong & died well.

Dale Ruff

Darrel: My friend Dale has long been one of my mentors. When I left my parish he asked, "What is your list of immediate and long-range retirement goals?"

Dale introduced me to the term "re-fire-ment," which he preaches with Calvinistic conviction. He means that we are to retire *to*, not *from*, something—some genuine extension of one's life skills and a new and exciting dimension to one's legacy.

Dale's own story is one of heartache and triumph. His first love died young, leaving him with two small children. A second happy marriage and two more children, a life filled with architecture, career development, travel, a family and church-centered lifestyle, and a dizzying range of community activities—a model for my living and re-firing.

Sandwiched between two churches—his Alpha and Omega churches—his story calls to mind the Master Builder themes of Henrik Ibsen: success and its vulnerabilities. The first church project was a tradition breaking architectural gem, a worship space in which I was fortunate to serve. The second project was a collaborative effort to replicate an ancient Norwegian stave church with a gentle soul named Guy Paulson. This project honored immigrant parents, and symbolized four decades of professional and personal growth for both men.

These two magnificent edifices are Dale's visual legacy. But beneath the visual lies a less visible legacy of the inner journey.

Dale distilled these lessons from his efforts:

- Death is a part of life.
- Have the humility to recognize that control is an illusion.
- Good is often wrung from bad.
- Attitude is more important than circumstances.
- Give back.
- Don't rest on your laurels.

Dale spends many days each year with Habitat for Humanity building housing for the poor. It is a natural extension of his life's work. I want to retire like Dale.

Wesley Jones

Lynn: My mentor, Wesley Jones, went to heaven last year—still looking for his shoes.

God put Wesley's buoyant spirit in my life forty years ago, and this man fed my faith enormously. Wesley was never flamboyant. But the glow of his radiant inner qualities lit up every room he walked into. Sparkling eyes. Warm smile. Rich resonant voice, flooding every conversation with encouragement. When I was still sprouting my preaching peach fuzz, Wesley called me all the way across Canada, from British Columbia to Ontario, "to speak at the opening of the senior citizen's home," he said. But mostly I think it was to feed my passion for ministry. And he published my master's thesis, *American Preachers in Canadian Churches*, "to help United States ministers in Canada," he said. But I think it was mostly to provide me a writing springboard.

Then in 1967, when I organized a major city-wide event, Wesley flew across Canada, east to west, to speak—and to mentor me in partnering with local media.

Wesley's main legacy, however, is his unflagging passion for world missions. One highlight of my life was attending the Congress on World Evangelism, in Manila, with Wesley.

Wesley planted churches in Canada, Indonesia, and Russia. And his influence extended into many other countries through short-wave radio. Until a long battle with cancer ended his travels last year, Wesley often revisited the churches he had planted on three continents.

Wesley spent several hours with twelve of us a few months before he died, reflecting on his approaching death. He smiled through his pain as we talked of ministry, life . . . and dying. He had no anxieties. None. We are all terminal, he reminded. But he asked us to pray for him . . . that he would effectively bear witness to Jesus in the circle of those who suffered cancer with him. We sat in his shade and drank from his cup that day.

The last few weeks Wesley scarcely left his bed. One day, Beverly heard some sort of noise in Wesley's room. She found him sitting on the edge of the bed with his shirt pulled partly around his shoulders, and he was fumbling on the floor for his shoes.

Beverly asked, "Hon, where are you going?" And Wesley replied, "I'm looking for my shoes. I need to go into all the world and preach the gospel."

"But, hon, you have already done that," Beverly responded, "So now you can lie down and rest." Wesley did lie down to rest and never got up again.

Yes, Wesley is gone from me physically. But his spirit still radiates fresh life. I want to leave this world with such a sense of peaceful closure on my heart.

Franke Messinger

Darrel: I first met Franke at a Senior University class on Great Books—and immediately recognized her to be an alert and growing person who was impossible not to like.

She and her husband, Paul, a retired medical doctor, had traveled the nation, and other continents, then settled in Texas to a full involvement in the local community—its youth as well as its adult citizens. She was the consummate cosmopolitan. Her two sons lived on opposite coasts while Franke and Paul lived between them in Texas.

Both had been in the "Finishing Strong & Dying Well" course that Barbara and I taught. In fact, Franke's participation was interrupted by a "bad cold" that turned out to be fatal lung cancer.

Paul called me to announce Franke's death and to ask me to conduct her funeral. I told him it would be an honor—and truly it was just that. Franke was 75.

At a memorial attended by their many friends and family, Barb and I gave her a course grade—posthumously—with the caveat that we did not grade on the curve or believe in grade inflation. Her grade was a splendid A. She had been a star student—a model of living vitally until her death, and a luminous victor over death itself. Shine on, Franke, we urged, shine on.

This bonus to our ministry was a double benediction on Franke and her life as well as on our ministry of vitalized maturity.

"Live fully to your dying day. Shine on in glory. God bless us everyone."

Lawrence Anderson

Lynn: Last, but definitely not least for me is the story of my own father, Carl Gustav Lawrence Anderson—known by all as Lawrence. In the weeks before he died he said to me, "It is past time for me to die."

Dad was eighty-five when he died in Moose Jaw, Saskatchewan, the day before Christmas, 1990.

When he left this world, no one lost an enemy. He was poor all of his life mostly because he always gave away most of what he had. Relationships always elbowed his possessions—and his ambitions—to the periphery.

Mom died two years before dad—Parkinson's disease. Her mental facilities left two years before her body did. Up until the last year, Dad cared for her, hand and foot, twenty-four hours a day. He rarely slept more than an hour at a time. Although he was tired, he still enjoyed life. Finally Dad could care for Mom no longer, so her last months passed in an extended care facility. But Dad went daily to read and sing to Mom that last year.

In Dad's final functional months, he was still the happiest man I knew. He laughed a lot, loved a good joke or an old story. He wrote poetry. I have a file of it, and there is not a sad song in the bundle. Life was precious to him, but he had absolutely no fear of death. Spoke of it often, and openly. On one of my last visits with him, before cancer took away his ability to speak, we sang a lot.

Remember my friend Frank who was alone? Unable to work. Broke. Aging, sick and dying. Frank who pounded his fist on the table. Well, my Dad didn't pound his fist on the table. He went out singing.

Dad finished strong & died well. Very painfully, but very well.

Chapter Sixteen

Grande Finale: Your Big Assignment

"The last of human freedoms is to choose your attitude regardless of your circumstances."

—Viktor Frankl, from a Nazi death camp

"I lost my dad in February, just before his ninety-fourth birthday. He was cogent when awake, right up to the end, but I wish he could have been more articulate about his feelings. I'm sure he was struggling, because a couple of times he said things like, 'I want to go out, but on the other hand I just don't know.' We tried to let him go wherever he wanted, but now I wish I had forced the talk a little."

—Jim Maxwell

KEY QUESTION: How will you, the patron, take stage and play your role in the S-aging drama?

T.S. Eliot wrote, "This is the way the world ends; not with a bang, but with a whimper."[1] No offense Mr. Eliot, but we don't believe every person's world needs to end that way. On the contrary we recommend the Big Bang theory for personal world endings. Regardless of your circumstances, you can design the last seasons of your life toward a strong finish.

Most dramatic presentations end with a grand finale. We have presented Life *as* Grand Theater while you sat in the audience. Now is your opportunity to step up on the stage and play out your own big, arm waving, grand finale.

More to the point: this is your Grand Finale, your big assignment. It is the all-important time to put this book's principles into practice in your own life.

You can do it! Many do. But to get started ask yourself these crucial questions.

Crucial Questions

1. *Am I willing to learn how to talk about my aging and mortality with family and trusted friends?*
2. *Am I willing to write my story?* (Including my life story and my Ethical will—my moral principled convictions.)
3. *Am I willing to design an Action Plan* with specifics for Wellness, Wholeness and Wisdom*?* Am I willing to design strategies and wishes for the later seasons of my life? This includes instructions to surviving loved ones: estate plans, medical directives, a living will and—just in case—hospice plans. (For a sample of Gilbertson's personal Action Plan see Appendix Two)

If you answer "Yes," then here are two top priority tips as you script and direct your finale.

Make sure to share your plan. Pass it along to significant persons in your life. (Especially with the one who might be widowed?)

Darrel: I freely discuss my plan with my wife, Barbara, and our three adult children.

Lynn: I have begun following Darrel's lead. For example, I have given my family funeral instructions and asked that my ashes be spread across the big hill overlooking the homeplace of my childhood years in Saskatchewan.

Commit to a Vitalized Life each day—to keep living fully until you die. This *can* be done! Recent poster children would be the late Pope John II and the aged Billy Graham whose effervescent spirits soar above the late stages of advanced age and monumental health challenges.

Help is Available

Besides your own talents and intuitions, you can easily find ample tools and coaching to help you plan your *Grande Finale.* For starters, noodle around the internet for a dizzying array of first class web sites. Start with: www.dying-withdignity.ca , which offers a gold mine of valuable tips (things like helping your family process your mortality—a huge one—plus travel for the physically challenged, medical concerns, living wills, wills and estate planning, writing and explaining last wishes, selecting hospice care—and many more.) This site also links to other helpful sites as well as to related governmental agencies and private organizations.

You will also find several interactive blogs on aging and dying which in turn steer you toward print journals and hard copy books. (For a list of books see a starter bibliography at the end of this book.) Help is at your fingertips. Now you are ready to begin.

Lay Out Your Plan

Get started by laying out a plan for the latter scenes of life—as well as for your death. Good *S-aging* plans and Grand Finales come in many shapes. But here are some first HOW TO steps to get you moving toward a plan that fits you.

Step One: Write your life history. Be sure to include emotional and spiritual dimensions.

Don't be afraid of faith language. Our appreciation of the language of faith keeps growing. Curiously, even in our overtly secular society, we can hardly talk without residual religious speech.

Step Two: Identify at least the three biggest lessons life has taught you.

Step Three: Spell out a short list of actions that amplify your life purpose.

Step Four: Act upon one of your legacy goals. (Whether age forty-five or eighty-five, begin now). If one fails, go on to the next goal. *Process* is more important than *product*.

Step Five: Follow through and revise or go on to the next legacy goal.

Lynn: Ron Miller, a retired executive from Procter and Gamble, serves on the board of the leader equipping non-profit I head up. He has helped keep the organization on mission, but also keeps my own personal S-aging life on point. Ron coaches me to periodically re-cycle these questions:

- What are your goals and aspirations?
- Where do you play?
- How do you win?
- What do you not do?
- What do you do next?
- When will you do it?
- What resources do you need to get it done?

Ron Miller challenges me to freshen the questions each time he recycles them by sharpening the specifics. You might find Ron's questions helpful in your own S-aging plan.[2]

Take Action

Of course, even the best plan means nothing without action. So set your specific starting date—*and start!*

Action 1: Talk

Communication is the principle. Silence is our enemy. Transparency our gift.

Darrel: I firmly believe more communication is better than less. So I talk to anyone who will listen as I process implications of my fatal illness. Even this book extends my voice.

My son, Todd, learned some helpful hints for the dying as he watched his father-in-law die, and now as he travels the journey toward death with his blood father. He warns, "It is usually quite awkward for those close to a dying person to raise the subject of the approaching death. It is also awkward for the one who is dying. People around you are walking on eggshells."

What can dying ones do to facilitate a healthier interaction with those around them? How can they put others at ease? Glen W. Davidson's classic book can be helpful here.[3]

First, to set the tone, Todd suggests three keys he has picked up on from his father:

1. Faith—authenticity
2. Fearless –vulnerable but undaunted
3. Fulfilled—a sense of completion, yet legacy

Todd offers these general suggestions for the dying person who wants to give his or her loved ones permission to talk openly about his or her approaching death.

- Prepare them mentally for you to be approachable on your deathbed.
- Help them find vocabulary to talk about it.
- Some gentle comments or questions you might ask are: You understand that I am seriously ill. Sometimes people feel a bit frightened around this kind of thing. How are you doing? Could we talk together about this? Do you feel at all frightened at times? With a follow up question: What can you tell me about how that feels?

Remember, it is usually the dying person who sets the tone.

Dr. Bruce Davis, former Gerontology professor at Abilene Christian University, offers the following assignment:

I give students an assignment like this: you have contracted the dreaded

Davis' disease that brings on sudden death, ninety days after diagnosis. You function fully until that ninetieth day—then die with the first ray of sunshine over the horizon.

Your assignment: write a list of all the things you want to do and say in those last

Ninety days. Usually, the class discussion leads to a very obvious conclusion: Why shouldn't we be doing every one of those things even though we are not terminal ninety days hence? Actually, we are all terminal! Until we accept that, we will likely not make the essential crucial life decisions nor will we live with the intensity and intentionality to live life to the fullest. [4]

Sadly when the loved ones and friends of a dying person don't feel free to talk about the person's condition, it is the classic elephant in the living room. Avoiding frank discussion with friends and family during the dying process denies us comfort, warmth. Somehow, the dying one needs to give permission to talk about the illness, closeness to death, and share the journey with those who are strong enough to participate.

Dr. James Knapp, gerontology professor from Southeastern Oklahoma State, agrees that "the death event and the dying process are still issues that we are not comfortable discussing," so he offers these pointed suggestions:

1. Let them know it is ok to feel sad (the pending separation from loved ones is cause for sadness).
2. It is okay to ask "why"? (God has broad shoulders and He can handle our questions).
3. Have genuine relationships (facades are removed when we understand the end is near. We can communicate in a more honest and complete way with those around us).
4. Grace becomes real (as we approach the end of life, the concept of grace is less of a church-based, abstract concept. It becomes the vehicle that will carry us into eternity).
5) Death is natural and expected (Just as God created the birth experience, He also created the dying experience).

A therapist friend, Joe Hale, reminds us that grieving is a process that cannot be hurried. He says all of life is change. All changes involve loss and every loss must be grieved. Otherwise, unresolved losses stack up in our hearts. We can get hung up in one or more of the so-called stages of grief: denial, numbness, anger, depression, etc.

Darrel: I agree with Hale. Barbara and I talk daily, set aside time, bring something interesting to our conversations. Nothing is unimportant; nothing is hidden. Barbara helps by opening just one emotional door at a time.

When we get together with our children, part of the visiting is honest talk about my mortality and the plans when I exit the stage. Whether through emails or phone or face to face—it is intentional and never accidental. They are open to this soul work.

Besides family, I have three email friends whose daily epistles are priceless. We also get together when possible, over the coffee cup, and discuss both the arcane and crucial happenings of our lives—including the big anticipation.

And of course, I keep my prayer lines open. Prayer on the patio each morning is basic to my life: For friends. For self. With all my wails of lament as well as praise and song, as I process my inner life—anxieties, needs, hopes and joys—with God-talk. My point is this: Say it. Give wings to your words. Be smart. Be patient. But talk!

Action 2: Write!
First, write out instructions for your loved ones, your physicians and your attorney.

Darrel: Make a paper trail. Make it legal. Make it visible. Do your homework earlier rather than later.

Put your funeral plans in writing. Draw up your will. Do and record the hard work of estate planning. It will be a great gift to your family and friends.

Repeat: leave no doubt about your terminal care wishes. Doctors and attorneys, spouse and children should never need to guess at your intent. Give directives to physicians and instructions to EVERYONE.

Even when we travel, Barbara and I take along a copy of our Medical Directives. We have updated our will. It was hard. But we included a Power of Attorney and Medical Power of Attorney too, in case both Barbara and I were incapacitated. We have distributed these documents and verbally made known our instructions wherever possible.

One cannot over-communicate this. As pastors we have witnessed hundreds of sad tales about slip-ups when intentions either were not put in writing or did not reach the right people. The case of Terri Schiavo is a sad example of this lack of clear communication.

Here is a skeletal map for writing these instructions:

1. The person you want to make health care decisions for you when you are unable to make them
2. The kind of medical treatment you want or don't want
3. How comfortable (palliated) you want to be
4. How you want people to treat you
5. What you want your loved ones to know[5]

To flesh out this skeleton, go to www.agingwithdignity.org/5wishes.

Darrel has written out his five wishes as follows:

Wish One: In consultation with, or if mentally incapacitated, with the medical power of attorney as directed by my will, I want decisions made according to my previously expressed thoughts.

Wish Two: when medical opinion is agreed that I have limited time to live, I do not want to be the subject of extensive therapy or treatment, but I do want to be cared for at home if possible, and then as medical procedures are necessary, in the hospital.

Wish Three: I want the liberal use of hospice knowledge of pain reduction.

Wish Four: I want to see my friends in person, or talk on the phone or receive emails, but do not expect to be surrounded by my family in death. No one should feel guilt if I die alone. I am with God.

*Wish five: A*s widely and clearly as possible, I will broadcast these wishes to family and friends, ask for prayers from my church and their prayer partners, and give written notice to all medical workers.

Addenda: Three additional wishes to the wish list include seeing my pastor (but not as a last rite), hearing Christian hymns, and receiving the Holy Communion (as food for the journey). My funeral directives will be with Gabriel's Funeral Home in Georgetown, Texas (a copy also with my church—Christ Lutheran in the same town).

Into thy hands I commend my spirit (from the words on the Cross).

Second, write out your life story—or "Life Review," to use Robert Butler's term.[6] This need not be done on paper. Some people use audio or even video recordings. Even more creative persons might express their life story in some other form (like painting, photo essay, woodwork, or construction project) that says, "This is my life."

For one giant example: sculptor Korczak Ziolokowski spent much of his life sculpting the Chief Crazy Horse Monument out of a mountain in South Dakota. Actually he died before it was completed and his family is still finishing the enterprise. Not long before his death Ziolokowski declared, "This is my story in stone."

Darrel: I prefer a more pedestrian medium. I write "Papa Letters" to my four grandchildren. They will know me if they take time to read them. I also write periodic page-length essays about a variety of topics that are windows on my soul. At least in part, they are my story in print.

I also consider writing this book with Lynn Anderson a direct outcome of my finishing strong activities. Something in me wants to share what I have learned with others for their use.

Lynn: I also write. I've authored several books, and even though I may not have always been conscious of it at the time, at least in part, my writing flows out of my *S-aging* process.

Third, write out what you have learned. Some of these specifics might be what you have gleaned out of the reflection process of sitting through this *Exit Stage Right* drama. But more importantly, spell out the key lessons learned across your own life experience.

Action 3: Choose!

Again we urge, Choose to be—and keep on being! Live life to its fullest on to the end. In the words of James Knapp, "Seize the Day. Realizing the finiteness of life, learn to live fully in each day you are given."

And William Carruth says:

He may live on by compact and plan
When the fine bloom of living is shed,
But God pity the little that's left of a man
When the last of his dreams is dead.
Let him show a brave face if he can;

Let him woo fame and fortune instead;
By there's little to do but bury a man
When the last of his dreams is dead.[7]

The point is this: don't leave a long vacuum of mere survival between now and your funeral! And start now! This is your real Grande Finale.

Curtain Calls

Lynn: I am learning and applying valuable things about my own unfolding drama of Finishing Strong & Dying Well—and my friend Darrel is my mentor and teacher.

Darrel: I am finishing strong, and am moving resolutely toward dying well. And my friend Lynn is a helpful partner in these later scenes of my *S-Aging* drama.

We together affirm that we have gained much from each other. We have both felt mutually affirmed. We keep each other moving.

Signed Covenant

We the undersigned recognize that unless we plan and act intentionally, we will drift aimlessly toward the end of life. We choose to finish strong & die well. We now turn our wills to this end and pray for each other to finish our lives vitally, fully alive with a sense of its meaning, and trusting to others who may have benefited by our contribution during our moment on the stage.

Darrel Gilbertson ______________________________
Lynn Anderson ______________________________
And now, what about you? ______________________________

Darrel's Final Bow

I lie awake on the recliner having just rearranged the garage to move my daughter's car in from the gathering storm. I have opened the blinds to allow me to see nature's pyrotechnic display. Flashes of lightning rip the black sky, and I hear the distant roll of thunder rumble on the other side of my front window. This severe thunderstorm is actually a metaphor for dying.

Thunderstorms and dying. The National Weather Channel moved us from an alert to a watch and then a warning that a squall line (I love that term) is moving in our direction. Will it weaken and fall apart? Will it gather itself like a demonic force and strengthen to third or fourth magnitudes? If so, how do we defend against it and protect ourselves from it? What *will* be the destructive level of this pulsating Doppler blip on our monitors?

Was this not like the waiting, watching and warning and strategies for defense that hector my thoughts daily? They say I am fatally ill. What can this thunderstorm teach me about its parallel storm—whose expected but unknown violence and chaos is just around the corner? I lay in the recliner and visualized my own inevitable death.

There *is* a small chance of dying from any given severe thunderstorm. By amateur guess, it may be less than a one-in-a-hundred-thousand chance. The statistical probability of thunderstorm fatality is not beyond calculation of meteorological and medical professionals who have developed formula for prognosticating these probabilities.

This evening's storm helps me envision several things about my own approaching death:

1. I accept that fact there is trouble ahead with my (our) mortality and choose daily rejection of the bonfire of vanities that plagues those in denial of death.
2. I harvest several helpful images of the squall line alert. Good information about lethality helps. A family emergency plan is essential. And I am encouraged to take an unsentimental approach to a catastrophic outcome—oblivion. (The weather cast even inadvertently defined oblivion when they reminded that a Force Five once caused a house with a family of five to simple disappear ten miles north of here.)
3. I see my own death at times. I know this prescience sounds absurd and in some ways it is truly impossible to visualize my own extinction. Yet,

> as I reflect on the gathering thunderstorm, I experience a great relief, if not comfort, from the thought that death will likely come to me like the chaos of a wild storm. Most people pray they will slip away during the night in their sleep but that is extremely rare. I visualize further, making a series of judgment calls. These calls may be pre-emptive and brilliant, or pre-mature and silly. (Just as it turned out to be unnecessary to move our daughter's car into the garage, because the storm skirted north of us hardly leaving a trace of rain.)

Some of those judgment calls I had already made: My Last Will and Testament is faithfully recorded. Funeral instructions are written down. A book has been prepared, conveying to any who might be interested the lessons life has taught me, and how suffering and relationships—even death itself—are my Master Prompters, my teachers.

I also visualize a surrealistic but powerful sense of my own countdown to death. As the hours, the minutes, and finally the first violent gusts (empty of rain) make my old house groan, I think hard about hospice, palliation, and finally the task of thanks and goodbyes to life's nearest and dearest persons. These images and reflections are unspeakably tender and mentally redolent.

I feel a very real catharsis of the soul, a therapeutic healing of sorts that defies adequate language (I usually do not lack words!). The mantra of "Finishing Strong & Dying Well" harmonizes well with the meteorological figure.

For nearly thirty minutes there arose a mystical, mysterious, core consciousness of languidly paced yet deeply meaningful visualization. I was cleansed and made whole. It was another glorious epiphany!

When it was over I fell asleep, my thoughts subsiding with the emotions and their peaks and valleys—like the storm outside my windows quieted and grew silent.

I awoke four hours later. The coffee pot beeped the end of its brew cycle. Instantly I was fully conscious of a pleasant sensation and recalled the thunderstorm and its boots-on-the-ground existential symbolism. I was consoled by the freeing and liberating sense I had taken from the experience.

Am I ready for my own death? Probably not. Will I finish strong? Is there a fair chance I will not finish strong but finish a bitter and miserable human being? God forbid. But never say never.

D-Day. I heard the Supreme Allied Commander, General Eisenhower, had done everything within his capabilities of making the Normandy landing a success. Nonetheless he also prepared a full news release in case the landing failed. That's how I feel.

I will do everything within my human capabilities to anticipate, face my death realistically and fully, and then strive to conduct myself with integrity and peaceful hope, surrendering to the reality of the final day of my life. But I may fail. And for that I write this apology or epitaph: *Sorry but I tried my best*. To God be all the glory.

—Darrel Gilbertson

Bibliography

Albom, Mitch. *Tuesdays With Morrie: A Old Man, A Young Man, and the Last Great Lesson.* New York: Doubleday, 1997. The riveting account of the encounter that "S-aged" both persons.

Becker, Ernest. *The Denial of Death.* New York: Simon & Schuster, 1973. A seminal text on the modern world's great thinkers and death as the core human problem.

Butler, Robert. "The Life Review: An Interpretation of Reminiscence in the Aged." *Psychiatry*, 26 (1963): 65-76.

Byock, Ira. *Dying Well.* New York: Riverhead Books, 1993. The best of the compassionate medical books on the topic of physical and social aspects of dying and death.

Davidson, Glen W. *Living with Dying: A Guide for Relatives and Friends.* Minneapolis: Augsburg Fortress, 1975.

Erikson, Erik and Joan. *The Life Cycle Completed.* New York: W. W. Norton, 1997. A posthumous work of Joan finishing the notes of Erik on the last chapter or stage of life which she identifies as the Ninth Stage producing "gerotranscendance." (sic)

Fowler, James W. *Becoming Adult; Becoming Christian.* San Francisco: Harper & Row, 1984. Fowler earlier wrote the famous *Stages of Faith,* but this book spells out in greater detail that pilgrimage of faith.

Goffman, Erving.*The Presentation of Self in Everyday Life.* Garden City, N.Y.: Doubleday, 1959.

Johnson, Richard P. *Twelve Keys to Spiritual Vitality: Powerful Lessons on Living Agelessly.* Ligouri, Mo.: Liguori Publishing,1998. A book written by a retirement inventory specialist and psychological and spiritual gerontologist. From him Darrel found the "Master Teachers" concept crucial to his own growth.

Kubler-Ross, Elizabeth, and Kessler, David. *Life Lessons*. New York: Simon & Schuster, 2000. A summary with a colleague of the original "Grief Stages" mentor's life lessons. Kubler-Ross worked with Carl Jung and died only recently in Phoenix.

Nuland, Sherwin B. *How We Die: Reflections on Life's Final Chapter.* New York: Vintage Books, 1993.

Silverstone, Barbara and Hyman, Helen K. *You and Your Aging Parent: The Modern Family's Guide to Emotional, Physical and Financial Problems.* 1982. Coaches middle-aged persons through the inevitable.

Terkel, Studs. *Will the Circle Be Unbroken? Reflections on Death, Rebirth and Hunger for Faith.* New York: Ballantine Books, 2001. A wonderful anthology of interviews with a full spectrum of people from celebrities to ordinary people.

Westburg, Granger. *Good Grief.* Philadelphia: Fortress Press, 1988. A primer on grief.

Appendix One

Gender Questions

Our first probes of the gender issues left us with many more questions than answers. A few examples:

- Do men and women view mortality differently and die differently? Why are the suicide rates of white males four times that of females?[1]
- Do men die twice—once when the career ends, and again when the body goes? I feel this question personally because I am grieving the loss of identity that goes with career. That is one encounter with mortality. Then having re-defined, re-discovered self, we face death again!
- Are women better at re-defining the self? Or what might this mean now that many traditional male roles are filled by women? Will a similar double dying afflict these new professional women?
- Are the different communication styles of men and women based on cultural patterns? Or are these differences inherent in the basic God-given psychological structure of men and women?

Possible tentative conclusions:

1. Although this is a relatively unexplored field of research, it appears that end-of-life matters are different for men than for women.
2. Men are especially vulnerable to mortality issues in spite of their tough and hard-nosed public face.
3. The authors feel strongly that they should speak directly to their own male struggles and feelings with finishing life and dying, then depend on women readers to make their differing or parallel observations.

An expert in the field of grief counseling, Joe Hale, offers the following websites for more help with understanding the differences in how men and women grieve[2]:

http://www.menweb.org/mangrief.htm
http://www.webhealing.com/
http://www.compassionatefriends.org/Brochures/understanding_griefnew.htm

Hale states that perhaps the greatest challenge in the way men and women handle grief is when one or more children of a couple die. Their grief may be magnified if there are surviving children in the family and their grief comes to bear along with the parents. Add to the equation the grandparents and their grief process, gender differences, age differences, and emotional makeup, etc., and you likely have a complicated grieving process.[3]

Appendix Two

Fill in the blanks.

I plan on becoming well physically

a. remaining fit by____________________
b. having fun by____________________
c. taking charge by____________________
d. influencing the course by____________________

I plan on becoming wise mentally

a. empowering myself by____________________
b. connecting with others by____________________
c. remaining open to change by____________________
d. challenging myself by____________________

I plan on becoming whole spiritually and morally

a. staying centered or focused by____________________
b. harnessing life's purposes by____________________

c. staying alert by ____________________

d. shining my light by ____________________

HELPS

1. Get with a friend or two and spend an evening swapping some stories about persons you know who finished strong and died well.
2. Write out a couple of your most inspiring stories:

APPENDIX THREE

Anticipating retirement, draw up two lists. This might be done anytime, but the best time is two years before you actually retire.

Things to do in the first three years:

1. ____________________
2. ____________________
3. ____________________

Things to do before I die:

1. ____________________
2. ____________________
3. ____________________

Endnotes

1. Glen W. Davidson, *Living with Dying* (Minneapolis, Minn.: Augsburg Fortress, 1975). Davidson inspired the Shakespearean "dying as theater" metaphor our book uses.

Chapter One—A Cast of Two

1. Erving Goffman, *The Presentation of Self in Everyday Life* (Garden City, N.Y.: Doubleday, 1959).

2. *Hope Network Ministries*, www.mentornetwork.org

3. Miroslov Wolf, "Speaking Truth to the World," *Christianity Today* (February 8, 1999). Also taken from conversation with Miroslov Wolf, Director of Yale Center for Faith & Culture at Yale Divinity School.

Chapter Two—Before the Final Curtain

1. Elisabeth Kubler-Ross, *On Death and Dying* (London: MacMillan, 1969), 154.

2. Mitch Albom, *Tuesdays with Morrie* (New York: Doubleday Dell, 1997).

3. The classic statement of Erik Erikson's Eight Ages is in his *Childhood and Society* (New York: W. W. Norton, 1963).

4. Ernest Becker, *The Denial of Death* (New York: Simon & Schuster, 1973).

Chapter Three—The Dangers of Denial

1. Soren Kierkegaard, *The Concept of Dread*, trans. Walter Laurie (Princeton, N.J: Princeton University Press, 1944).

2. Ernest Becker, *The Denial of Death* (New York: Simon & Schuster, 1973), 175.

3. Becker, 175.

4. Romans 5:5 NIV.

5. Ecclesiastes 12:1-5 NIV.

6. Psalm 90:12.

7. Joan M. Erikson, *The Life Cycle Completed* (New York: W. W. Norton, 1997).

8. This discussion stems from views expressed in James Fowler's book *Becoming Adult, Becoming Christian: Adult Development and Christian Faith* (New York: Harper & Row Publishers, 1984), 30-37.

9. Willie Nelson, "You Remain," *The Great Divide* (Lost Highway Records, 2002).

Chapter Four—Set One: The Pathway of Ages and Stages

1. Susan Weissman, *Victor Serge: The Course Is Set on Hope* (Brooklyn, N.Y.: Verso Press, 2001), 121.

2. Flannery O'Connor, *The Complete Stories* (New York: Farrar, Straus & Giroux, 1979), 225.

3. Among these sources are the French developmental school language of the Four Ages, the American developmental school led by the Eriksons, the historic "Seasons of Life" literature

in Western Literature, *The Layman's Guide to Life II* by Bob Buford, and, Darrel's favorite Old Testament "gerontologist," Ecclesiastes.

4. Bob Buford, *Halftime: Changing Your Game Plan from Success to Significance* (Grand Rapids, Mich.: Zondervan, 1994).

5. Peggy Lee, *The Best of the Singles* collection, Peggy Lee Music and Media Trust (Hollywood, Calif.: Capitol Records, 2003).

CHAPTER FIVE—Set Two: The Card Game of Circumstance

1. Quoted by William C. Kerley, "Finding Faith Again," *Mission* (November 1972): 6.

2. Hints of this appear in John 1:4, John 10:10, Romans 9:10-17, Philippians 1:6, 1 John 5:1-1.

3. Quoted from the movie, *Brother Sun and Sister Moon*, 1972.

4. Charles Zanor, "Live Life to the Fullest: Enjoy Every Sandwich," *Newsweek*, August 9, 2004.

CHAPTER SIX—Set Three: The Trapdoor of Perceived Permanence

1. Paul Simon, "Old Friends/Bookends," Columbia Records, 1968.

2. Rami Shapiro, *The Way of Solomon* (San Francisco: HarperSanFancisco, 2000), 175.

3. Nicholas Perricone, *The Perricone Promise: Look Younger, Live Longer in Three Easy Steps* (N.V. Perricone M.D. Ltd., 2004).

4. Bob Buford, *Halftime: Changing your Game Plan from Success to Significance* (Grand Rapids, Michigan: Zondervan Publishing House,1994).

5. John Richard Neuhaus, *As I Lay Dying: Meditations upon Returning* (New York: Basic Books, 2002).

6. Robin Marantz Henig, "Will We Ever Arrive at the Good Death?" *The New York Times,* August 7, 2005.

CHAPTER SEVEN—Meet the Master Prompters

1.Miriam Makeba, African singer and political activist, quoted in *The Whole World Book of Quotations*, "Wisdom from Women and Men Around the Globe Throughout the Centuries," by K. and R. Petras (Addison-Wesley Publishing).

2. *Jack London Reader* (Philadelphia, Penn.: Running Press, 1994), 242.

3. Richard P. Johnson at a 2002 Tucson conference on "Fearless Aging." See the website for Senior Adult Ministry, Johnson Institute (Be sure to include the "P" in your search—as in Richard *P.* Johnson).

CHAPTER EIGHT—First Master Prompter: Suffering

1. From Shakespeare's *Hamlet,* Act 3, Scene 1, spoken by Hamlet.

2. Genesis 50:20 NIV.

3. 1 Corinthians 9:27.

4. Philippians 3:14.

CHAPTER NINE—Second Master Prompter: Relationships

1. www.quotedb.com

2. *Lutheran Book of Worship* (Minneapolis: Augsburg Fortress), 48.

3. David Augsberger, *Caring Enough to Confront* (Scottdale, Pennsylvania: Herald Press, 1980).

4. Stephen R. Covey, *The Seven Habits of Highly Effective People* (New York: Free Press, 1989).

5. Matthew 5:9.

6. Covey, 1989.

7. See Story Map appendix, "Tell Me Your Story," 196.

8. "Desiderata" written by Max Ehrmann (see website for the confused history of this poem).

Chapter Ten—Third Master Prompter: Dying

1. Brewer, G. C., *Brewers Sermons* (G. C. Brewer, 1928), 288-289.

2. Author unknown.

3. G. C. Brewer, 1928.

4. Psalm 90:12 NIV.

5. Betty Freidan, *The Fountain of Age* (New York: Simon & Schuster, 1993), 121.

6. George Eliot, *Middlemarch* (New York: Barnes and Noble Books, 1996), 276.

7. Ernest Becker, *The Denial of Death* (New York: Simon & Schuster),175.

8. Psalm 46:1.

9. *A Tribute to Ebon C. Ingersoll,* by Robert G. Ingersoll.

10. From a teaching program by Jack Hayford many years ago; check his website for further information on his ministries: www.jackhayford.org

11. For helpful direction on relationship completion suggested by hospice, see Ira Byock, *Dying Well: Peace and Possibilities at the End of Life* (New York: Riverhead Books, 1997), 139-40.

Chapter Eleven—Sub-Plot 1: Mortality

1. Studs Terkel, *Will the Circle be Unbroken? Reflections on Death, Rebirth and Hunger for a Faith* (New York: Ballantine Books, 2002), 21.

2. James W. Fowler, *Becoming Adult; Becoming Christian* (San Francisco: Harper and Row, 1984). Fowler earlier wrote the famous *Stages of Faith*, but this book spells out in greater detail the pilgrimage of faith.

3. Betty Freidan, *The Fountain of Age* (New York: Simon & Schuster, 1993), 111-12.

4. www.meaning.twu.ca

5. 16th Sonnet written on his blindness by John Milton. Year of composition uncertain (probably 1655). First printed in *Poems* in 1673.

6. 2 Corinthians 4:7.

7. Helen Lemmel, "Turn Your Eyes upon Jesus," first published in *Glad Songs* (British National Sunday School Union, 1922). Lyrics inspired by a gospel tract by Lilias Trotter that included the following words, "So then, turn your eyes upon Him, look full into His face and you will find that the things of earth will acquire a strange new dimness." Source: www.cyberhymnal.org.

8. From *Sports Illustrated*, November 17, 2003.

Chapter Twelve—Sub-Plot 2: Legacy

1. Percy Bysshe Shelley, "Ozymandias," a sonnet published in 1818.
2. William Shakespeare, *MacBeth* 5.5.17-28.
3. Sinclair Lewis, *Main Street* (New York: Signet Classics, revised 1998).
4. Psalm 90:17.
5. Ecclesiastes 1:11.
6. Ecclesiastes 3:1f.
7. www.mentornetwork.org
8. Joan Erikson, *The Life Cycle Completed* (New York: W.W. Norton, 1997), 127.
9. Ibid.
10. Matthew 16:25, NIV.
11. Psalm 127: 1-2, NIV.

Chapter Thirteen—Sub-Plot 3: Identity

1. Darrel's note: the stages/seasons are "frontloaded" by which we mean most occur in the First Age before approximate age of twenty-five. Little work was done with "elderly patients or people." This is a serious criticism of the epigenetic and faith schemes.
2. James W. Fowler, *Becoming Adult, Becoming Christian* (San Francisco: Harper & Row, 1984). Fowler earlier wrote the famous *Stages of Faith*, but this book spells out in greater detail the pilgrimage of faith.
3. Shakespeare's *Hamlet*, spoken by Polonius, 1.3.78-80.
4. Beth Rosenwald, *Baltimore Daily Record*, January 4, 2003. She refers to *Managing for Results*, by Peter Drucker.
5. Ecclesiastes 1:2.

Chapter Fourteen—Encore: Players Look Back

1. Robert N. Butler, "Age, Death, and Life Review," originally appeared in *Living with Grief: Loss in Later Life*, ed. Kenneth J. Doka (Hospice Foundation of America, 2002).
2. In a sermon August 8, 2004, as reported by the *Washington Post*. Presidents Bush (both) were in the congregation.

Chapter Sixteen—Grande Finale: Your "Big Assignment"

1. www.brainyquote.com
2. Ron Miller, retired vice president of Procter Gamble and on Hope Network Ministries Board of Directors.
3. Glen W. Davidson, *Living with Dying* (Minneapolis: Augsburg Fortress, 1975).
4. Email from Dr. Bruce Davis, former Gerontology professor at Abilene Christian University, May 2006.
5. The Five Wishes (www.agingwithdignity) challenges aging persons to put their wishes in writing and communicate them to family and physicians.
6. Robert Butler, "The Life Review: An Interpretation of Reminiscence in the Aged," *Psychiatry* 26 (1963): 65-76.
7. William Herbert Carruth, "To Dream Again."

Appendix One

1. National Institute of Mental Health website: http://www.nimh.nih.gov/suicideprevention/suicidefaq.cfm

2. Joe Hale, www.coachjoe.com, joe@coachjoe.com. Joe is available to do Loss and Grief seminars and workshops for churches, as well as coaching for individuals, families, and groups.

3. Email exchange between Anderson and Hale.